Essential Information After High School Graduation

Essential Information After High School Graduation

Michael Anthony White

VOX GEEKUS

The events and conversations in this book have been accurately chronicled to the best of the author's rather sound mind and exceptional memory.

All information presented henceforth is to be regarded purely as personal opinion of the author based on their own experiences, and is not to be considered professional or legal advice, direction, instruction, or guidance of any manner whatsoever. The publisher and the author assume no responsibility for the actions of the reader.

To the maximum extent permitted by law, the publisher and the author disclaim any and all liability for errors, inaccuracies, omissions, or any other inconsistencies herein.

Copyright © 2022 by Michael Anthony White
Cover art by Michael Anthony White

All rights reserved. No part of this book may be reproduced in any manner whatsoever without written permission except in the case of brief quotations embodied in critical articles and reviews.

Second Edition, 2023

ISBN 978-1-7377921-4-7 (hardcover)
ISBN 978-1-7377921-6-1 (paperback)
ISBN 978-1-7377921-5-4 (ebook)
ISBN 978-1-7377921-7-8 (audiobook)

Published by Vox Geekus

CONTENTS

DEDICATION viii

1
Operating from Outside the Bias-sphere

2
Culture Shock Absorption

i Us Californians 12

ii "Only in New York!" 19

iii Travel Broadens Horizons 28

3
Money Train-ing

i I Was Homeless Once 34

ii Losing Interest in Cars 44

iii If You Can't Pay Cash, You Can't Afford It 49

iv Shooting for the Bottom 52

CONTENTS

v ▍ It's Never Too Late If You Care Enough   61

vi ▍ How We Did It   73

4
Don't Never Stop Learning

i ▍ It's Worth It   92

ii ▍ It's Not Worth It   98

5
The Selling of Science and an Unstable Pyramid

i ▍ Lies and Lousy Science   102

ii ▍ Some Better Science   107

iii ▍ It's Okay, They're Natural Killers   115

iv ▍ Stoners' Disappointment   118

v ▍ My Diet Is Trendier Than Your Diet   121

vi ▍ Keeping Your Wits   126

vii ▍ Next Moves   128

6
That Digital Abyss

i ▍ A Gift and a Curse   132

CONTENTS

ii | Mob Mentality and Cowardice at Their Finest 139

iii | Not of Our Own Devices 152

7
Political Parties Aren't Much Fun

i | They're Apparently Not That Good at Their Jobs 158

ii | We're Apparently Not That Good at Voting 163

iii | Party's Over 170

8
=

i | Ethnicity or Epidermis? 176

ii | The Legendary Battle of the Sexes 181

iii | Some People Have No Class 194

iv | Of Indignation and Martyrdom 198

9
Onward

ACKNOWLEDGMENTS 206
ABOUT THE AUTHOR 207

For all the teachers that stepped outside the bias-sphere, and the students who chose to follow

1

Operating from Outside the Bias-sphere

I always felt patronized during high school assemblies when guest speakers tried desperately to impress the student body.

My aversion grew more intense on the occasions in which they'd struggle to pander with social or fashion trends, drop popular TV show references (which they frequently botched), or even attempt to adopt the slang of our generation.

They often embarrassed themselves; we always saw right through them.

I also wasn't a fan of the opposite.

At times the angle was played that they *didn't care* whether or not we thought them clever enough to hear out before they babbled on with some condescending cookie-cutter advice.

Regardless of how they chose to play it, what often followed were idle threats of future failure in life if we didn't load up with college debt as our first step into adulthood.

This delightful little ritual of indoctrination was repeated biannually.

Guest speakers were commonly introduced as experts in their fields, nevertheless I was *certain at the time* that none of their propaganda would need to be embraced in order for me to land a successful career.

Now that I'm older and wiser and have reflected on those memories many a time, I must confess:

I was absolutely correct.

Per the doctrine of many, I'm still not an expert in anything because I have no college degree.

I could easily say, "That's their opinion, and they can eat it."

Yet if I did, I'd be wrong; that's not their opinion.

That's their *presumption*.

expert

noun
/ EK - spərt /

1. One possessing a high level of knowledge or skill regarding a specific subject or area.

Intentionally playing the arrogant card in turn, I've provided some support points below:

1. I'm a Senior Support Technician with nearly 25 years' hands-on experience, and earn a 30% higher salary than that of the average college graduate. I also avoided the debt that comes with a four-year degree, which according to an article published in 2021 can now cost over $325,000.

2. I've been a part-time professional musician for over 20 years.

3. I've been brewing ale, cider, and mead for nearly a decade while regularly being compensated for my brews during public events.

4. I've been designing and crafting custom wooden board games since high school, with some going for over $100.

It would appear I'm doing just fine.
I'm clearly an expert in *many* fields.
Let the reality that I have lived free of debt for years, have several wise investments well in place, and remain ahead of schedule for retirement serve as proof.

(Ok, that's enough. It's time to come clean.)

A lingering question remains regarding the authenticity of both those speakers' *and* my expertise:

To what *extent* are we experts in our fields?

Without offering in a willing, civilized manner any further details or intricacies — without considering the multitude of pertinent variables that have great potential to bring clarity and credibility to the matter, we're forced to proceed by uncivilized social means at best.

Assumption.

Extrapolation.

Implication.

Insinuation.

Profiling.

Stereotyping.

All of these are prime ingredients in the mortar full of failsauce being ground up by none other than the pestles of our own individual biases.

As to expose some misleading elements, I hereby offer some clarifications on my prior points:

1. A national survey from 2020 truly indicated I earn a 30% higher salary than that of the average college graduate, but when compared only to those who majored in Computer Science, this figure falls to 6%. I had exploited the full scope of the survey to embellish my success. To add extra flavor to my proclaimed superiority, I'd also performed the verbatim web query, "Most expensive colleges in the USA," to really lay it on thick. I found an article from 2021 listing the top 50, and scrolled down to the college with the highest annual cost to start crafting my argument from there. When I later queried for the most *affordable* universities in the USA, plenty were in fact found with annual dues of less than $7,000. This means that if one first acquires their Associate's degree at a city college before transferring to a less expensive four-year university, a Bachelor's in Computer Science can be acquired for quite a reasonable price. I'd intentionally omitted that little tidbit.

2. The statement, "I've been a part-time professional musician for over 20 years," isn't false, but still misleading. My first paid gig was a two hour event in 1999 for $40. Since then, I've worked only a few events every year, most of which have been local performances.

3. I do have several years of experience brewing beverages, but at home. Homebrewing is a hobby, not a profession. As for being compensated, I'm a member of a homebrew club whose compensation is that of free admission to our local annual beerfest. If we pour our own beers at the homebrewers' club booth for half the duration of the event, we're free to wander around and sample as we please. Despite accolades from friends and strangers alike while being *very proud* of my work, I've never actually sold my homebrew because it's illegal to do so in the USA. I've also never worked at a brewery.

4. With regard to designing custom board games, it too is a hobby. I recently donated one of them for a silent auction where it went for over $100... but I've never directly sold one for more than $60.

My wife Kelly and I do truly live free of debt, and are indeed ahead of our retirement schedule. I suppose that should support my claim of expertise well enough.

Notwithstanding, embracing self-serving bias by using the dishonorable tactic of generalizing my accomplishments (while obscuring choice details) allowed me to *really* yuck it up and boast, resulting in a skewed profile.

One need not lie in order to deceive.

This vile practice is the bread and butter of many corporations, politicians, and quite predominantly... The Media.

All three frequently rub off on society, breeding bias.

Though there are still numerous elements and counterpoints enough for the validity of the term *expert* to be debated for perhaps the length of this book, I personally have an aversion to that dirty little word.

debate

verb
/ də bāt /

1. To argue in a formal manner.

Argue, huh? That doesn't sound like the most constructive of activities.

argue

verb
/ ärgyoo /

1. To provide reasons or cite evidence with the goal of persuading others to share one's view.

2. To exchange or express opposite views, typically in an angry manner.

Some synonyms for "persuade" are: *entice*, *brainwash*, and *convince*, which don't exactly resemble benchmarks of morality, and an "angry manner" is anything but conducive to... being conducive, so to what end shall points be argued? What is the goal of a debate?
To agree on every detail?
To get along?
Compromise without violating freedoms?
Live and let live?
Defeat the opposing side because it's not one's own?
Are we seeking fairness? Justice?
...*Vengeance?*

That's not my idea of a good time, nor does it sound like an ideal way to bridge gaps. It rather sounds to me like a fantastic method of creating more fissures by way of stubbornness and spite.

I feel this way due to a personal bias.

When I was in high school, classroom debates often consisted of the room being split in half. Each side would elect the most popular students as their speakers, and they'd *have at it.*

It didn't matter if what was said held any truth or had a solid foundation; it became a roast that was based on fabrications, rumors, and semantics.

In the end, it was all about which popular kid could rip on the other the hardest.

Who delivered the *best* package of insults wrapped in the most clever passive aggression? That's what always determined the winner.

Spoiler Alert: Political debates between *cough* "adults" are often just as sophisticated — rife with biases and plagued with prejudices.

Biases can perpetuate the omission of data and exterminate compromise. They can obscure details and kiss off truths.

I've always tried to identify mine, and *do* something about them instead of saying, "Well, *everyone* has biases..." and leaving it at that: an excuse.

Acknowledging my own bias toward the word, I try to avoid *debating* anything these days.

Instead, I've adopted the habit of offering in a willing, civilized manner... some observations from various perspectives that I've picked up over the years. Many are those I can only *wish* had been revealed to me during high school.

Using a carefully crafted approach, I've discovered that even the loudest hot seat topics within our online society today that often end in stalemates, angry rants, and — at times, that cowardly behavior of unfriending — can instead be discussed with dignity and grace.

It's amazing what happens when one operates from outside the "bias-sphere."

A rather effective technique is to imagine one's written words are being audibly spoken to people face to face in the same room. Suddenly our responses become more than just text on a screen.

I find civility can be easier maintained when addressing majorities and minorities alike with the same level of respect I hold for myself, my friends, and my family.

So, what has been determined here?

Does my personal success without a college degree prove those "expert" guest speakers useless?

Does my personal success make *me* an "expert?"

Here's a basic shot at détente:

Although an individual might fit the dictionary definition of an expert, this does not guarantee them to be of any assistance to you personally — in such cases, this phenomenon does not necessarily invalidate their expertise.

Finally, an objective statement! It's neither accusatory nor derisive toward either party; it welcomes further reasoning with additional variables, allowing flexibility without aggression.

First, do no harm.

I am indeed an expert on the history of my own life, including the lucid recollections of what has succeeded, and what has failed.

The holding of immediate college enrollment as a requirement for success being thrust down my throat during high school affected me greatly and in a destructive manner. There were *so many other* pertinent aspects of life that I wish had been mentioned before graduation day because they would have helped me out exponentially.

I graduated high school in 1997 at age 17. I'm now 41 years old. I've brought forth some of the hottest tips and insights that I've picked up since, as I genuinely believe they'll be of great and timely benefit to many others as well.

Culture Shock Absorption

2

Us Californians

I was born in Huntington Beach, California in 1980, and have fond memories of my time spent living on Brookhurst Street. The beach was just a 15 minute ride in a Radio Flyer from our apartment.

A child of mixed ancestry, I enjoyed moderate diversity at Eader Elementary School alongside several classmates hailing from The Middle East, India, Japan, and Mexico.

We all got along effortlessly, and I wasn't the only one who liked hearing those students talk about their families, home life, favorite foods, and games.

My family would frequent Coco's Bakery & Restaurant on weekends, rarely going without an order of their fried zucchini.

Claim Jumper was another favorite, as their old western theme was far more immersive back then. The managers even used to walk around wearing chaps and a star-shaped sheriff's badge during their shifts.

Celestino's was a local Italian butcher shop that made *the best* beef jerky I've ever tried, and I can still taste it. I miss it.

Living only 20 miles from Knott's Berry Farm *and* Disneyland, we took advantage several times a year.

Parking at the latter was two dollars, and our family of four at the time walked through the gates for a grand total of less than half the price of a single adult ticket today.

It was affordable.

I lived in Huntington Beach until age six, and can still remember the relaxing vibe. After all, it's on the coast. That's usually a sure thing.

Moving a few hours north, Atascadero would be my next home from '86 to '89, where I'd adjust to country life. We rented a house my grandpa had purchased upon moving west from Indiana in the late 1950's. He still lived locally, so we got to see him often.

I learned about gardening, scraped up my limbs from riding bikes with friends every chance I could get, and heard a large number of Midwestern accents for the first time.

The accents of those living in town varied greatly, and at that age I couldn't really identify which were from Indiana, Tennessee, Oklahoma, Texas, Georgia, or elsewhere... I only knew they were all fun to hear because they were so different from what I was used to.

Come 1990, we ended up moving to what would become my longest and most familiar hometown, Solvang, California.

We already knew of it well, us being SoCal residents and Solvang being a popular vacation destination.

I was so excited to start school and make some new friends here, but a certain unfortunate event starts taking place inside most humans right around age 10.

When left unchecked, strongly misunderstood emotions fueled by new hormones coursing through young bodies may reel out of control, allowing unkind actions and destructive behaviors to thrive:

Peer Pressure. Egos. Prejudice. Discrimination.

Puberty.

Moving to Solvang in fifth grade was kinda lousy at first. I was a newcomer who had just joined a society of young humans in a small town who — for the *majority* of them — had spent the best of grade school together and were now comrades with an established history.

Many weren't keen on welcoming outsiders at that age.

I daresay it was *traumatic.*

I had for the first time become a target. A misfit.

My favorite musicians were Weird Al and Spike Jones. That made me a dork.

My favorite book genres were Science Fiction and Fantasy, and I was really into Math and Computers. That branded me a nerd.

I loved quoting TV shows, movies, and talking about video games. That proved I was a freak.

There's something about being a social outsider that's been a cliché element flaunted in stories as long as I can remember, and from my experience is a blatant example of art imitating life:

Outsiders find each other, and stick together.

The easiest friends I made were other kids who had *also* recently moved to town.

We related to being treated like trash on the basis of dressing and speaking differently, and having interests that didn't align with those of the long-time local kids.

Many of us remained close all throughout junior high.

Culture shock isn't exclusive to traveling outside of one's country. It can occur county to county, city to city.

Once high school rolled around, I clicked with even *more* outsiders, and we all grew closer as the student body grew more venomous with age.

I was popular only among fellow band geeks and computer geeks, but something happened by the time Senior Year rolled around.

Some of the students who had berated and ousted me years prior suddenly *began* to treat me like a human being. I never sat down with any of them for a heart-to-heart as to why, and I didn't need to.

Adolescence is a brutal stage. Watch any film about glorified high school life, and you'll see the same story told time and again:

Snot-nosed kid hits puberty, is allowed to act terribly toward others due to less than optimal [or complete lack of] parental guidance, and becomes popular by stepping all over the protagonists — *the outsiders.*

When crisis peaks and the plot climax arrives, this antagonist is then exposed as a coward, a fraud, or both. Along with their cronies or other supporting villains, they grow a conscience and suddenly acknowledge that the outsiders have been treated with unfounded vitriol.

Everybody comes clean, buries the hatchet, emotional growth is achieved, roll credits.

Late high school is a time where things get real. Children become adults. One discovers the kind of person they are.

My experience of being mistreated so frequently by the overall student body had been so off-putting that I didn't even care to show up to the Senior Awards Ceremony.

Unbeknownst to me, my parents had been sent a school letter in the mail that revealed I was to receive an award during the event. Wanting to keep it a surprise, they *insisted that I go* when the time arrived.

The audience was disrespectful, rude, and shouted jeers at the unpopular kids who received awards that night.

I was already miserable 30 minutes in to the ceremony and wanted to leave when suddenly I was called up to receive a "Recognition Of Excellence In Music" award. It was a flimsy signed piece of letter paper with a corporate bank sponsor's logo printed larger than my own name.

Not exactly feeling recognized, I finally had my wish to leave granted by my parents as they too were under the impression that was that.

It was not.

The next day, I found out the ceremony had ended with a segment of *special* awards.

I had been honored by United States Marines appearing in full uniform to present to me the "Semper Fidelis Award For Musical Excellence" as an accomplished performer and soloist.

This award was granted to just 15,000 students nationwide.

Since I was no longer present when being called up to accept the award when it was announced (with reportedly grand applause), I was contacted the next morning during first period to quietly retrieve the framed award in an envelope from the Administration Building.

Throughout that day, quite a number of Senior Classmates (who'd rarely acknowledged my existence for four years) had expressed they were completely confused why I'd left before ceremony's end, and offered bona fide congratulations upon seeing me.

Some shouted sarcastic deprecation from afar in the hallways to mock my accomplishment, but very few jumped on their bandwagon.

Quite a contrast to prior semesters, that.

True colors had been shown by Senior Year, and distancing had taken place by many upon revelation of who was authentic and honorable, and who was... well, not.

It was a bittersweet end to my high school experience.

My band geek and computer geek friends are still very close with one another, as the strength of our camaraderie that kept us going was intense.

We had banded together to get through what was necessary.

All these experiences affected me in a manner that *to this day* cause me to wonder certain things about every person I meet in life.

What kind of childhood did they have?

Were they an outcast in school?

Were they the popular fraud that changed their ways and stopped feeding their ego?

...Are they struggling desperately to feed it still today?

It's not the healthiest long-term practice to suspect such things, as it too breeds bias and feeds insecurities. Since my school days, I've always had to make a conscious effort to keep myself in check as to avoid defeatism and negativity.

Traumatic indeed.

A few years after graduation day, I moved to San Diego in search of finer job opportunities. That was the first time I felt I'd been "thrust" into a busy, big-city working world.

I was on my own in a completely new place, but it was adventurous; I was enjoying a thrilling dose of excitement.

One of the most common stereotypes about the people living in popular big cities — especially those in California and New York — is that they're all stressed, pretentious, arrogant, and rude.

Living in San Diego for four years while also frequenting Orange County *and* Los Angeles County for business and pleasure, I met some of the friendliest strangers on streets, in restaurants, hotels, bars, and workplaces.

I've found no glaring excess of rudeness per capita spewing forth from these cities.

In fact, the *sources* that I consistently recognize perpetuating the highest volume of such stereotypes are TV shows, movies, and the general public.

Several magazines and newspapers even publish annual articles highlighting what they claim to be the rudest cities in the country based on surveys and public input.

Public input.

When I think about the people I've heard circulating this rubbish firsthand, a common quote comes to mind that one would *think* should serve to invalidate the claim by nature:

"No, I've never *been* to [big city name], they say it's full of nothing but rude people, so why would I ever want to go *there*?"

Let's analyze that gem, shall we?

If they've never been for themselves to see if it's true, and *they are* the people who are saying it, then...

Yep. One to ponder, alright.

The two most common places in the USA that I hear being mentioned in this manner are Los Angeles, and New York City.

Whenever traveling out of state and it's revealed that I'm visiting from California, more often than not the other party will fire back, "Oh, are you from Los Angeles?"

I still meet several people who are under the impression it's also the State Capitol.

I suppose I understand. Los Angeles *is* a large city, popular, and often in The Media. It's not as if I'd expect people to guess I'm from a small Danish tourist town with a population of 5,000.

I'm not alone, though. My wife Kelly's relatives all feel my pain, as they hail mostly from Rochester, New York, and can relate to these patterns and stereotypes all too well.

Los Angeles is just a mere fragment of what makes up our state. New York City, likewise.

Much can be learned by taking a glance at a map.

"Only in New York!"

Numerous movies set in the Atlantic Northeast feature foul language that's completely over the top. It's desensitizing to the point that the words lose their once powerful impact, feeling as if they perhaps no longer hold any meaning at all.

Thanks to such films, those who've never been there might be convinced that everybody in New York City is rude, crass, and curses like a sailor.

On the contrary, some of the kindest, most polite, and helpful humans I've met were in Manhattan.

My wife and I had the pleasure of visiting in 2015, at first spending a few nights near Times Square.

Day one, Kelly heard a pedestrian publicly curse at a taxi who'd almost hit them by driving up on a curb.

It was understandable.

Later, we heard somebody swear once to themselves when reading a newspaper on the subway.

That's the *only* foul language I recall hearing the entire visit.

As far as rudeness, we saw *one* public spectacle that I could never imagine taking place back in California...

We had just finished a profound visit to pay our respects at the 9/11 Memorial & Museum, and decided to stop by Shake Shack on Murray and North End before heading back to the subway.

We arrived right as the lunch hour hit, so we got to see how a restaurant in New York City handled the serious crowd.

It was our first Shake Shack experience, and I'll never forget it.

To summarize, the line was out the door no less than 40 people long, yet we were still sitting down and eating our food less than 15 minutes later.

That's professionalism.

After enjoying our meal we walked back to the subway, and that was the first time we'd experienced "the droves."

There's a scene in the film *Crocodile Dundee* where Michael is shown walking in downtown New York City for the first time, *overwhelmed* by the sheer density of people all around him traversing streets and crosswalks.

From the experience Kelly and I had, that scene was completely accurate.

The crowds in San Diego and even Los Angeles are sparse in comparison. Though no *small* number of people reside or operate within those cities, they're peppered comfortably throughout roads and walkways.

A couple blocks away from Shake Shack, the immediate group of pedestrians we were closely walking with had grown to about 60 people.

Generally quiet small talk was being made by many, the closest of which being a couple to our right. We'd gathered from their conversation that they were surely coworkers.

They spoke with strong accents, both dressed in conservative professional attire — the woman in a crisp long business suit, the man wearing a white shirt with black slacks, tie, jacket, and yarmulke.

He had just lit up a cigarette and had hardly taken his first drag when a female pedestrian ahead of him let out a quick double cough.

"Aw, come on lady, *get* ova' yaself, **we're outside!**"

His coworker quickly snapped at him, calling him out.

"Oh now *that* wasn't necessary, did ya have to word it like that? *That* was very rude!"

After a sigh, he proceeded sheepishly and genuinely:

"Aw geez, look lady, I'm sawry, she's right... ya' didn't deserve that. I've jus' had a lousy day and took it out on ya right then, it's my fawlt, really, I didn't mean ta snap at ya, I'm sawry..."

The woman who'd coughed remained calm, and having seen the untimely misunderstanding, slightly turned her head and accepted his apology. She also replied that she was sorry if it sounded like she was coughing for spite, but she'd sincerely just had something caught in her throat. She'd had a long day too, and empathized with his short fuse.

They both bade each other a good afternoon, and after a few seconds of silence, his coworker commented, "Hah! I love it. Only in New York!"

Several [presumed] locals in the group as well as Kelly and I laughed warmly in good-natured support.

I'd never seen such a thing on the West Coast.

Rudeness appeared to be sparse in Manhattan, and in that specific instance it was quickly called out — not with the intent to seek vengeance, but understanding.

Everybody we happened to ask that week for directions or suggestions showed great pride in their city. As busy as they were, they still took care to offer a concisely definitive answer with confidence before quickly moving on.

That's what I felt was the essence behind the "New York Minute"... strict timeliness, but with sincerity.

We also soon learned that the locals were quick to speak frankly, often in a hilarious manner.

The "Subway Construction Worker Incident" was a favorite example:

The Subway Construction Worker Incident

SETTING: Kelly and I had boarded a subway train to return to our hotel after lunch one day, taking our seats near a tall thin construction worker. He was standing up in full orange reflective gear, complete with hardhat. An elderly woman also sat nearby. After a few minutes, a youth hardly looking to be a high school freshman had boarded the train as well, blasting loud music rife with profanities and crass themes on an external bluetooth speaker. *Something* was announced over a nearby P.A. speaker, but had been drowned out by his music.

[loudspeaker: ...*will not be stopping at ...eenth street. Transfer instead at... avenue gate... ank you.*]

KELLY
(whispering to MIKE)
Great. Did you hear any of that? Was that *our* stop that's closed?

MIKE
(shrugging, speaking quietly)
No idea, I could barely hear it.

KELLY
(to CONSTRUCTION WORKER)
Excuse me, sorry to bother you... did you happen to hear that? We're heading back to our hotel by the Port Authority but we couldn't hear which stop was closed.

CONSTRUCTION WORKER
(responding loudly in the direction of THE YOUTH)
Yah, me neith'a, I couldn't hearit ova' the friggin' beat-box music!

THE YOUTH
[only slightly embarrassed for being called out, looks the other way with music still playing loudly]

CONSTRUCTION WORKER
(looks at MIKE and KELLY, continues)

Yah, it's 14th that's been closed a couple o' days, so no problem, ya' fine all the way.

KELLY AND MIKE
Thanks a lot! Thanks much!

CONSTRUCTION WORKER
No problem, (laughs) yah I could hawdly hear it myself!

[as train quickly comes to its next stop, THE YOUTH gets up to exit without a word or glance, his music still blasting]

CONSTRUCTION WORKER
(loudly)

YAH, HEADPHONES, Buddy. GETCH'A Some!

ALL
(laughing)

ELDERLY WOMAN
Oh thank you, I'm so glad you spoke up, that's rude to blast music so loud that people can't even hear anything else.

                    KELLY
                (still laughing)
Yes, thank you again for your help! Sorry for laughing, we're visiting from Central California, and are just surprised — we don't hear too many people speak up like that back home.

                ELDERLY WOMAN
                (laughing as well)
That was great, this was like a moment in a Seinfeld episode!

              CONSTRUCTION WORKER
HAHA! Yeah, that's right, I gotch'er Larry David right heah!

                      ALL
                (more laughter)

ESSENTIAL INFORMATION AFTER HIGH SCHOOL GRADUATION

I admit to my fellow West Coasters that it was so cliché, the story sounds fabricated. I still maintain that's how it happened, verbatim — I kid you not.

Another moment that stood out regarding locals' willingness to help would occur just days later when we attended the main event of our visit: One of Kelly's lifelong friends was getting married at a hotel near Pearl River.

We ended up taking a bus from Port Authority Midtown that would drop us off just two miles from the wedding. A pickup from a private transportation service had been arranged to take us the rest of the way.

Just as we were exiting the bus, Kelly received a call back from the service in question to be told they'd decided it wasn't worth their time to give us a ride anymore. They were 20 miles away and had no other service requests in our area.

They had officially requested to cancel our pickup.

With warranted irritation, Kelly responded, "Really? We're already here and you're not coming?... Fine then, cancel it!"

At that point, I'd offered to carry both suitcases and walk the remaining two miles, when someone at a nearby stop sign had overheard Kelly's exclamation.

They pulled up to the curb in their large old SUV and shouted out the window to Kelly, "Where ya goin', honey?"

Kelly and I were taken aback, so after a stunned moment of silence, the woman called out again.

"Looks like yer waitin' fa' a ride that isn't comin', so where ya tryin' ta go?"

Kelly quickly mentioned our destination, and without a blink, the stranger tells us, "No problem! Hop in. I can get you there in 5 minutes if you don't mind the smoke..."

She ashed a lit cigarette nonchalantly.

Kelly gave me a concerned look as I returned a confidently grateful one, complete with a raised eyebrow and a side smile.

"The rear door should be unlocked, just pull tha handle hawd... you can toss ya bags whereva' they fit back there, sorry for the mess."

"Oh, no, thank you so much for helping us out!"

We got in the back seat, and the woman introduced herself as Mattie Rosina. She was the retired widow of a firefighter who had worked at a station in Harlem.

When hearing about how our scheduled ride had dumped us, she shook her head.

"Well *that's* not very professional, they should be *ashamed...*" calling the service out.

She asked how we'd enjoyed our trip so far, and we told her of how much fun we'd been having on our first visit to the city. We mentioned how helpful and generous everybody was, and how they'd all been so quick to assist with directions and offer recommendations. We also summarized the Subway Construction Worker Incident, and she just laughed and nodded, saying, "That's the way it is in New York, we say what's on our mind."

She asked how long we were staying in Pearl River, and we explained it was just for one night. We'd then be going back to a different hotel located in the Upper East Side for a few days before flying back home.

"Oh yer gonna have fun, it's much more quiet than Times Square in that part'a town. Compared to where you were before, it's very laid back — but listen, honey..."

She grew serious, lighting a fresh cigarette.

"Just some advice fa' you two kids, if ya go out at night, ya **stay** where it's populated, **stay** in the lights and **stay** with a group of people. Don'tchoo go out aft'a midnight when it gets dark if ya' don't know the area. Be smart, and if ya ever feel like you're in danger or you're being followed, ya both walk **right** into the next open doorway and ask to use a phone. Call a taxi and tell them you need a ride ta' the fire station..."

She then gave us the exact address.

"Give them the street and the Ladder number, but **don't** say it's in Harlem. Some taxis are too scared to drive there at night because they think it's too dangerous. They don't realize it's not like that anymore. Just give the address, and when ya get there tell'm Mattie Rosina sentcha' and they'll take good care o' ya..."

By that point, we'd reached our destination. When we tried paying her for her time and generosity, she wouldn't have it.

She instead smiled and furled her brow at Kelly, saying, "Oh honey, I can't take any payment, you were hawdly out of my way. Keep that and give it to charity or someone in need."

We thanked her wholeheartedly, and she drove off with a smile and a nod as she wished us well, ashing her cigarette once more.

Warmth and kindness abound.

Our trip was incredible, and by week's end we had both agreed that there was a rich feeling of camaraderie amongst the locals in New York City.

Was it because of the density of the population? The frequent close physical proximity of other people?

Maybe it was due to the recent tribulations the city had been through.

Having spent just one week in Manhattan, that I can't say.

What I *can* say is that there was a special feeling on the streets and among the people that was powerful and supportive and real.

I've not felt that in any large city on the West Coast.

I can't recommend a visit to Manhattan strongly enough to anybody who wants to immerse themselves in culture, history, and of course to see for themselves how the city really is.

Several things are certain: I'll never forget Mattie, that construction worker, or the peaceful resolution of the misunderstood cough on the streets of the Financial District.

I would never describe the people of New York City as pretentious, arrogant, or rude. As a matter of fact, our experience proved to reveal quite the opposite.

I ♥ NY.

Travel Broadens Horizons

To act with haste in the search for the absolute rarely ends with an objective truth. It's easy to allow unchecked emotions to fuel extrapolation of nominal facts, and end up with nothing more than a heavily biased conjecture *masquerading* as a personal truth.

Kelly and I had moved to Tigard, Oregon in 2006 where we lived for four years. It was there that we rode out the infamous real estate crash of 2008.

We'd tried constantly to meet new friends, chatting with other couples and making small talk about where we'd moved from.

A couple of times per week, we'd be showered with animosity toward "us Californians" for moving north in substantial numbers and destroying the economy. We'd be personally blamed for making it near impossible for locals to afford to buy a residential property in their own hometown.

I was once told to go back to "People's Republic Of California" where it was accused of being so miserable that one would, "...have to be an alcoholic to *tolerate* life in that state..."

After enjoying these audible pleasantries for nearly the 30th time, we finally learned how to skate the subject.

If the question of where we were from had been asked directly, my wife would reply that her family was from upstate New York, and I'd say some of my family had lived in the Pacific Northwest for years (which was true).

That seemed to exempt us from any further SoCal witch-hunting.

It was sad, and it seems this prejudice hasn't waned.

Years after we moved back to Solvang, a relative sent me an article from an Oregon news network via email in 2015 in which they were reporting a new trend.

Round stickers featuring the shape of California with a red slash through it had started to commonly appear on real estate signs. This was to serve as an indication that the owners wouldn't sell to anybody from the state.

The clip featured interviews with local real estate agents and home owners explaining that though *some did* hold such a disposition, it was suspected that an excess of the stickers were being affixed to signs by "punks and... hipster types that enjoy graffiti... that's an activity for them to do other than go out and get a job to make the money to afford these houses."

The article also clarified the reality that 70-75% of new residents were actually *not from California.*

Can you imagine if Kelly and I had operated with an equally terrible bias against *Oregonians* in our first few months of living there?

Biased Extrapolation Against Oregonians

#people met/week	#anti-CA remarks	rudeness ratio
4-6	2	33-50%

If we embraced extrapolation with this severely closed-minded amount of data, we would be proclaiming that 33 to 50% of Oregon residents were inherently rude, and practiced antipathy toward Californians.

That sort of incriminating deduction is inexcusable.

Sadly, it's commonly practiced.

Let's look at some objective, *unbiased* numbers for that same time period:

#people met	Oregon population	% of people met
52-78	3.676 million	.00001 - .00002

We met roughly one to two, hundred-thousandths *of one percent* of the population.

That's… not a lot.

Here's the objective reality: Without asking 3,675,922 or more people [at the time] what they thought of Californians, any attempted conclusion would be nothing more than a shamefully gross assumption.

There are many expressions regarding the nature and repercussions of assumption, *none* of them being all that particularly reflective of intelligence.

I once provided tech support in 2005 to a body shop owner calling from Florida who was requesting assistance reinstalling all required software from scratch. He'd just rebuilt his entire shop for the third time in two years due to storms and flooding.

When I apologized for what he'd gone through, his reply floored me:

"Yah, it's rough, but at least it's not as bad as livin' out there in California! Y'all got earthquakes!"

That sounded *absurd* to me, but so does the fact that I've met countless Californians who have sworn never to visit Kansas, Oklahoma, or Texas, because they're afraid they'll get caught in a tornado during their arrival.

Where on earth people got the idea that earthquakes occur *that* frequently, or that air traffic controllers habitually send flights right into the eye of a storm is beyond me.

Every state in the USA has its own unique culture. By being mindful of personal biases and resisting stereotypes, one may easily turn a potentially alarming culture shock into a fascinating, pleasant learning experience.

Assumptions will only bring about fallacies.

3

Money Train-ing

I Was Homeless Once

I never had the privilege of taking Home Economics in high school. Try that I did, I always ended up on the waitlist.

Tragically, many schools today have stopped offering the course altogether.

Looking at the American economy as well as the habits of our society, it's a shame it wasn't (and isn't) universally required.

Just one year after my graduation, I'd happened upon a time in which my roommate had abruptly moved out of state to live with family.

This left me with only a couple of weeks to find a new place to live.

We'd been renting a single room for $500 per month from a house in Santa Barbara County.

I had a less than stellar job, bringing home $1,000 per month after taxes. Consequently, that served as a decent start with $750 left after paying my share of rent.

Unfortunately, I'd been less than wise with my money, going out often and spending about 50% of my paychecks on entertainment.

I'd go to the movie theater a couple times per week while loading up on snacks and refreshments. I'd eat fast food or pizza nearly every day, and buy several DVDs, CDs, and video games with every paycheck.

When I *did* go grocery shopping, my cart was usually filled with low-quality frozen boxed meals, instant ramen noodles, and prepared foods housed in cartons or cans.

A massive failure of budgeting *and* nutrition, that.

If only I'd gotten into Home Ec!

After my roommate vacated, my only remaining possessions were a bed, small dresser, TV, my video games and other aforementioned media, my clothes, and my car.

I ended up finding a small storage unit for $25 per month where I stored my few belongings, and had started living out of my car with a suitcase in the trunk.

Still keeping my lousy job, I ended up joining a local gym for a mere $20 per month as to have access to a daily shower.

Hardly anybody knew that I was quietly living out of my 1981 Chevy "Citatio" hatchback (the letter *n* had long fallen off), parking in unlit lots or obscure side streets every night to sleep.

This is not recommended.

After a couple weeks of this routine, a friend of mine named Jay had spotted me looking quite exhausted by my car one evening after work. There he learned of my not-so-debonair living arrangements.

After giving me an earful about not reaching out to friends for any help, he worked out a deal with his parents to rent out a spare bedroom on a short-term basis.

They ended up renting that room to me for over a year at the generous price of $175 per month. They could have gotten $300 for it at the time, but were glad to offer the friendly rate.

They had been *responsible* with their money.

Not taking this generosity for granted, I turned those consequences of my youthful pride and stubbornness into a lesson of wisdom, and exercised discipline and perseverance to avoid *ever* having to live out of my car again — though I'm grateful to have had at least that.

Rent, or more properly, *housing*, is by and large the greatest expense in a personal budget. It's not uncommon to hear of people spending well over 50% of their income on housing in several areas of California.

With the exception of a few astronomically priced ZIP codes, this is not necessary — it is a choice.

There's a common and heartbreaking pattern regarding the financial status of the average American:

When one loses a job, they're quite often in dire straits and panicked the very first week; they're in crisis and flat broke shortly after receiving their final paycheck.

They were living in a large house.

They'd always flaunt the latest smartphone.

They were always sure to post pictures of the newest large-screen TV mounted on their wall.

They traded in their car nearly every year for a current model.

They could *clearly* afford to dine fancily and frequently, as they'd post several photos on social media every week showing off beautiful platings at fine restaurants.

Some would even travel coast to coast or to Europe several times a year.

That ain't cheap.

Public conduct had given the impression that these many folks were all well-off and financially stable.

In reality, they simply had great credit.

Had.

In short, what they likely had was great debt, and were living paycheck to paycheck. They didn't *own* much of anything. Their creditors did.

I was no different for many years in this respect, as financial discipline is no easy accomplishment.

According to The Federal Reserve as of spring 2021, total American household debt is at a record $14.6 trillion dollars. To demonstrate that number as an *average,* we could say that every individual citizen in America over the age of 18 has about $56,000 of personal debt.

Kelly and I found that a great advantage to our budget has been choosing to live in the smallest dwelling that is reasonable.

We do not currently have, nor plan to have any children at this time; it's just us and our two cats, Aeris and Crono. There's no reason outside of luxury for us to require anything more than a single bedroom apartment to comfortably live at the moment.

That's our personal decision, and it's different for everyone.

Kelly has a local job working in an office, and I've worked remotely at home in the field of tech support for decades.

Living rooms usually have corners, and they've served well to accommodate my small desk in every apartment we've lived.

Don't get us wrong, we'd absolutely *love* to get into a house and enjoy a yard to grow our own produce, have a spare room to acoustically outfit as a small recording studio, a decent sized kitchen with newer appliances that actually function well, and laminate flooring instead of old matted carpet.

A living room designed to our liking would also be nice, so that we can have friends and family over *comfortably* instead of huddled on small creaky chairs at a dining room table with wood-patterned plastic coating...

But this is what we can afford right now.

There's a common misconception about renting an apartment versus buying a house, in that a house is often touted as *the ultimate sure investment!*

I've often heard the argument that every penny you spend renting a place to live is like flushing all that money down the drain — whereas a house payment is like putting every penny into the bank.

A dangerous misconception, indeed.

The Dangerous House Payment Misconception

The market is affected by plentiful elements, many of which are volatile and fickle; buying a house anytime for the sake of it is *never* a "sure investment," and making payments on one is absolutely *not* like "putting every penny into the bank."

When renting an apartment, you pay the monthly price of rent, plus usually three utilities.

Using Santa Ynez Valley as an example, the lowest priced listing I see today (9-8-21) for an available one bedroom studio apartment is $1300 per month.

Electricity, water, and gas will total about $200 per month, provided you aren't running an air conditioner or any other large appliances.

It's true: Everything mentioned above is an expense. Nothing is invested. That's $1500 per month "down the drain" for housing.

Apartment Example Summary:

Monthly:	Expenses -$1,500	Invested +$0
30 Yrs*:	Expenses -$540,000	Invested +$0

*for ease of this example, your rent and utilities magically did not increase over the 30 year period.

Now let's look at the costs of buying a house:

When purchasing a house, you have the honor of making a mortgage payment which includes the principal, interest, property tax, insurance, and quite likely PMI.

PMI (Private Mortgage Insurance) is a fee charged to most all buyers who provide less than a 20% down payment on the house. The lender basically sees them in a less than confident light, and PMI is charged as protection in case the buyer (that's you!) defaults on the loan. The rate for PMI is typically 0.5-1.0% of the value of the house.

More space requires more utilities. Those will be going up for sure.

Maintenance of the foundation, flooring, walls, wiring, plumbing, roof, landscaping, appliances, fixtures, and any emergency repairs will be your responsibility now as well. No more calling the owner or manager to fix things! *You're* the owner. *You are* the manager.

Using Santa Ynez Valley as an example, the lowest priced single family home I see listed today (9-8-21) is a two bedroom house on a small lot for $650,000.

Let's also say you have an excellent credit history and FICO score, qualifying you for a rate of 2.9% on a 30-year mortgage loan.

Using the low average of current county rates for the size of your home, property tax comes to $4,290 per year, and property insurance is $960 per year. These are worked into your mortgage payment by the bank for convenience.

Realistically, you won't have a 20% down payment of $130,000 cash at the ready, but you manage to scrape up the bank's required minimum of 3%, $19,500. You'll be stuck with PMI until you've paid back 20% of the principal and refinanced your house, which is typically about eight years into the loan. We'll pretend you qualify for the lowest PMI rate, 0.5%. Again, the bank courteously incorporates this into your mortgage payment.

As mentioned, you now pay higher utilities than in an apartment, such as more electricity, more water, more gas, and now sewer and trash. Using the low average, we'll say they total $300 per month.

Finally a plus: Since you have a small house, your maintenance and repair costs will be mild compared to most. Generously using the dream figures of the lowest average for a two bedroom home in the Santa Barbara County, this comes to $8,000 every five years.

This brings us to the end of this pleasant fiction, where we can now analyze these totals and determine how much of this wild trip has been an expense versus an investment.

House Example Summary:

Down Payment:	Expenses	Invested
($19,500 total)	-$0	+$19,500

Monthly Payments:	Expenses	Invested
($3,560.84 total)	-$1,755.29	+$1,805.55

30 Year Total*:	Expenses	Invested
($1,281,903 total)	-$631,903	+$650,000

*for ease of this example, your utilities and other costs magically did not increase over the 30 year period.

Presuming you pay off the loan as scheduled, you will have spent a total of $1,281,903 between principal, interest, tax, insurance, PMI, utilities, maintenance, and repairs.

That means outside of the $650,000 investment, you've flushed an *additional* $631,903 down the drain over 30 years.

$1,755 per month in expenses.

Suddenly, the apartment's expense of $1500 per month doesn't look all that bad in comparison.

"...well, I've INVESTED in a $650,000 house, and now it's 30 years later. I can sell it for BIG BUCKS!"

Can you?

Keep in mind that in this example, you bought that house in 2021 at an extreme *high* of the market.

Many condos in Santa Barbara County sold for over $400,000 in 2007, but after the infamous real estate crash of 2008 their value had harshly dropped to under $250,000.

Their value now in 2021 is *hardly* back up to $400k; that's zero profit over 14 years for the unlucky buyer who purchased in 2007. Not only that, but they'll have spent well over $300k in expenses by the time their loan is paid off!

We're currently due for another potential economic crash, so those properties are likely to lose a nasty chunk of their value again in the upcoming years.

If you bought high, the return on your investment likely won't be stellar anytime soon.

This example also used *dream numbers* from the lowest averages of expenses in California. Likewise, many other elements weren't even factored in, such as inflation, utility price hikes, and potential property tax and insurance increases after refinancing to ditch the PMI.

It's true that if a 15-year mortgage were considered, the interest lost ($314k) could have been roughly cut in half.

(That is, if you could afford a mortgage payment of over $5,000.)

In addition, there's nothing stopping you from paying off a mortgage faster if your budget permits, despite that other misconception that it's better to *keep* your mortgage around… for the tax benefits.

It is not.

Using our above scenario, the first year of mortgage payments results in you handing the bank a little over $18,000 in interest.

It's an expense. It's *gone*.

When tax time comes around, you tell the federal government, "Hey wait, I paid the bank $18,000 in interest. Help me out here!"

They answer, "Oh sure, why not. You're in a 25% tax bracket, so we'll give you back 25% of your paid interest."

You then get an extra tax return of $4,500, and are overjoyed with a check in your hand at first — and *only* at first, because you can perform basic arithmetic. You come to the realization you've paid the bank $18,000 in interest so that the government would give you $4,500 extra toward your tax return.

You've… lost $13,500.

Now, this has all been one fun hypothetical example of doom and gloom, so let's look at a *positive* scenario:

In 2012, one could easily find a three bedroom house in the Santa Ynez Valley for a mere $300,000.

Pretending that you had been wise with your money, we'll say you had saved the $60,000 cash to put 20% down and avoid PMI.

Being as the house was a fair price, you paid less property tax and insurance and were able to afford to pay it off in a fraction of the time compared to a property over twice the price.

Today, many of those three bedroom houses are being listed for over 1.2 million dollars after only nine years. Even with zero improvements having been made to them, buyers are getting into bidding wars and paying well over asking price.

Volatile and fickle.

Everybody's situation is different. All details should be taken into consideration before figuring whether or not to purchase a home.

People have to decide for themselves if they can afford to rent a large house for the mere luxury of extra space.

Depending on the market, a three bedroom house with four to six roommates who happen to get along swimmingly might just *be* more affordable than several individual apartments.

When in doubt, one of many safe options is to stay in a small, low-cost apartment or rented room while contributing to a very diverse selection of choice investments. This is beneficial in saving up for a massive down payment, or to eventually pay cash in full for a house when the market is low.

That's exactly what Kelly and I are striving for, and it's working faster than expected now that we're free of debt.

Buckling down in a small apartment to minimize our housing cost has been the *second* best decision we've made to benefit our budget.

Not spending 50% on entertainment would be the first.

Losing Interest in Cars

Kelly and I own a 2019 Toyota Corolla. We bought it new and paid it off in 2020.

We were hesitant at first because there's a lot of advice going against the purchase of a new car, *ever*.

"The value goes down thousands of dollars the moment you drive it off the lot."

It does indeed. It becomes a used car.

This *would* be a substantially relevant factor if we intended to trade it in or sell it in the near future.

We do not.

We intend to keep it and drive it for several hundred thousand miles.

It's new. It's ours. We're the only ones who have driven it and we know *exactly* how it's been treated.

This provides remarkable peace of mind.

Our last car was a 2005 Toyota Corolla and we just sold it this year — not because it was driven into the ground or had any issues but because we didn't need two cars anymore.

Aside from the green LED clock sporadically fading in and out, *nothing* was wrong with the car after 220,000 miles. No major parts had failed.

The only items that had been replaced were those to be expected from normal wear and tear: Spark Plugs. Belts. Batteries. Bulbs. Tires, et cetera.

There *was* a rear right lens replaced, but only due to being shattered from a parking lot hit-and-run. (By the way, thanks much whoever you were.)

We had such a great experience with our first Corolla, we bought another one. So far, it's just as satisfactory.

Some friends prefer other makes and models, and they too often run for over 200,000 miles when they're taken care of.

Maintenance is key. It's always more affordable to keep a vehicle in shape than to let things go and end up with a domino effect of additional wear and tear from disregard.

Yet, what's reasonably priced for one person might be out of reach for another.

Enter the next commonly largest chunk of a personal budget: *transportation*.

I'm not going to discuss favorite sports and luxury vehicles, or driving for pleasure here — that falls under *entertainment*.

I'm talking about functional transportation as a required cost of living.

One needs a place to live, and I've already mentioned a vehicle is ideally not recommended for such purposes. That being said, most people do find it necessary to travel from their place of living to that of their employ, and on occasion a farmer's market or grocery store. These activities give us the ability to earn money to pay for housing, and purchase food as to prevent ourselves from starving.

This *is* recommended.

I have a few friends that live in New York City who profess they've not owned a vehicle in years, don't *need* one, and don't want the expense.

As of this month (September 2021), the price of taking the NYC Subway is currently $2.75 for a single fare or $127 for a monthly pass.

That's an *excellent* deal.

The NYC Subway is incredibly efficient, and during our own week-long visit we learned that it could even be much faster than a taxi depending on where you're going and what time of day it is.

Not every city's public transit system is as efficient, and many rely purely on buses for transit. Though usually not as timely as a rail system, this still serves as a feasible option.

Both Los Angeles and San Diego offer monthly passes for $100. In less populated cities, transit systems are usually priced even lower due to a smaller service area and more limited schedules, such as in Santa Barbara or the Santa Ynez Valley. They're $52 and $42.50 respectively.

With any public transit system, travel time varies greatly with every city and location. With the exception of NYC, the majority of them are *not* the promptest method of travel.

You might want to bring a book.

Traffic withstanding, riding the bus system in San Diego 15 miles each direction to work and back five days a week would regularly take well over an hour *each way* — at times nearly *two* hours depending on routes and number of stops.

Driving a car that distance outside of rush hour might only take 20 minutes each way.

The compromise?

Instead of paying $100 per month to take the bus, you'll pay an average of $370 per month to use your own vehicle just for your work commute.

Time is money.

The cost of driving is more than just a few gallons of gas. You have to pump that gas into a vehicle, and burn it.

Vehicles aren't cheap.

As of 2021, the IRS has defined the current mileage rate as $0.56 per mile.

Naturally, many statistical averages were used to arrive at this number, so yes: In reality your cost will absolutely be lower if you drive a Corolla instead of a Land Cruiser.

The true cost of driving a vehicle includes gas, oil changes, all other scheduled maintenance, repairs, registration, insurance, parking fees, toll road charges, and storage if necessary.

Much like purchasing a house, buying a new car can be pricey, draining one's money in the form of interest over the course of many years.

Unlike the principal of a house, a car is for all intents and purposes an expense.

I've definitely kept my budget in check over the years by driving used cars, but one must be wise about it.

I wouldn't suggest going out and buying the cheapest used car in the local paper for $1,500. You might end up with a 20 year old economy car with 378,000 miles on it and a stench of cat urine permanently infused into its rusty frame.

That's a marvelous way of paying through the teeth for replacement parts every couple weeks, and it's not worth your money in the long run to go that cheap. Leave those cars for high schools and colleges to purchase (or be donated) for shop class.

I've spoken with a lot of people about cars. I'm not *into* cars, and I don't have any dream car that makes me drool like a little kid every time I see it...

(Well okay, other than a '67 Chevy Camaro RS/SS, but I'm pretty sure that's everybody who grew up watching *Better Off Dead*.)

I've only talked about cars so much because of going through excessive grief with old junkers that I should have ditched years prior.

Consistently, a large number of friends and family have had the greatest bang-for-buck success when purchasing dealer-certified used cars that are about three to five years old. These cars have been driven just enough to take a nice chunk off the price without having suffered substantial wear and tear. They also come with a limited certified used warranty.

Searching within my county, several listings are available today for 2018 and 2019 Toyota Corollas with under 50,000 miles for $16k. They're only a few years old, and that's several thousand dollars off the retail price with many dealers advertising less than a 2% APR loan. Working even a minimum wage job, one might have that vehicle paid off in a couple years if they aim for it.

You don't want to pay interest on *anything* ideally, but especially not a vehicle. Never forget that it's an expense, not an investment.

If you want to save money, great deals can be found on less expensive used cars, and they'll run just fine for several years.

Keep in mind, once it surpasses the 20 year *or* the 250,000 mile mark, **it's getting fairly grizzled.** It might be time to sell it before it stops running completely at which point you have to *pay* to have it hauled away to a junkyard.

That's not a good day. I try to get rid of them before that.

Kelly and I had a plan to pay our new car off in less than a year when we purchased it, and we exercised discipline to accomplish that goal. We paid less than $320 in total interest by doing so, and that's fantastic.

We'll be able to pay cash for our next one, and that's even better.

iii

If You Can't Pay Cash, You Can't Afford It

I may have said once or twice that my wife and I live free of debt.

I've actually mentioned it four times so far because we're so excited about it. It still feels surreal.

We had been *in* such debt for so many years, we're still coming to the realization that we're half-way stable.

We're still recovering from the trauma.

We'll never go back.

Since I've already pointed out the absurd havoc that interest can wreak over a long period, that saves us some time.

Now realize that the average credit card interest rate is over 16%.

That's the average.

New credit card accounts are often 18.99% or higher, and you can expect some retail or department store cards to be over 25%.

If you buy a new $3,000 gaming laptop on that credit card and take a year to pay it off, you've now paid $3,421.

The hook is simple: "Buy now, pay later" is inherently addicting.

It's instant gratification.

Some can resist the temptation, and others have to go through a painful lesson for decades before realizing that if you can't pay cash, you can't afford it.

Literally, you can't.

You don't own it, the creditor does. If you can't finish paying for it in a timely manner, they'll end up taking it back after keeping the interest you've paid.

That's called an expensive rental.

Volumes of material that dwell on the importance of avoiding credit card debt have already been published, so I'll get to the part about using credit cards *responsibly*.

That's right, I use credit cards regularly yet I'm still free of debt.

I use them for both security and for discounts.

Extremists will try pounding it into everybody's head that credit cards should never be used for any purpose.

Those people aren't enjoying an extra 5% off almost everything at Target.

Yes indeed, I use my Target credit card every time I shop there because [as of writing this, anyway...] you get an additional 5% off almost everything you purchase from their store or website. There are very few exclusions that mostly involve some pharmacy services, restaurant merchants in stores, some mobile carrier services and a few others I can't remember.

I don't work for Target, I just shop there occasionally.

As with most credit cards, if you pay the balance off in full the first month, you don't pay any interest.

It's my personal rule set in stone: **If I don't already have the money in my checking account to cover what I want at the time of purchase, I don't buy it.**

Kelly and I both have credit cards that offer 2% cashback for every purchase anywhere, and even more at gas stations.

Regarding the use of credit cards for security, we've done so for quite some time.

About eight years ago, we were fans of using a debit card for every purchase. It's convenient, and promptly takes the money directly out of the account for easy balancing of our checkbook. It's also insured against theft.

The problem is this:

If it *is* compromised, your checking account is frozen until you can make it into your banking branch to sort things out. From that moment, you're stuck withdrawing cash in person from inside the branch or writing checks until a new debit card is mailed to you.

It's flabbergasting, the amount of businesses that still don't accept checks in the year 2021.

As for carrying large amounts of cash, I've acquired quite the aversion to it due to an incident back in 1990.

The week after my 10th birthday, my parents drove me to the nearest Toys R Us so I could spend all the birthday card money I'd received. Somewhere between the car and the checkout line, I lost my wallet.

There was over $110 in there, and whoever found it didn't turn it in.

I've rarely carried cash since.

Another personal bias.

Inconveniences being what they are, the clincher for Kelly and Me was having our debit card numbers compromised twice in the same year.

One theft was traced to a local restaurant chain, and the other from a gas station.

A thief is a pathetic waste of life.

It was a big enough inconvenience pulling out cash and using up checks for those couple weeks to convince us to start using our credit cards for added security.

That's when we started receiving offers for cards providing cashback or discounts on every purchase.

We've hardly touched our debit cards since.

Used responsibly, some credit cards can provide significant benefits and perks as long as you simply stick to your budget.

Used haphazardly, they can cause a lifetime of hurt.

Shooting for the Bottom

Kelly and I moved back to California in late 2010 after living in Oregon for four years.

Though we'd met some great people there and were able to spend time with family, the timing of the job market after the 2008 real estate crash didn't work out in our favor and we found ourselves returning to SoCal.

As a remote employee working at home, I was able to retain my same job while Kelly started her new career in real estate appraising.

We'd successfully ditched our habit of excessive restaurant spending and had reeled in all unnecessary entertainment costs as to put a chokehold on our self-inflicted crippling debt.

Both of us had really started to pay attention to every little detail of our budget. We analyzed our own behaviors as well as those of the average Americans around us.

Spending habits, strengths, vulnerabilities of ours, and those of strangers were silently studied in passing in order to hone our financial discipline.

Certain things were harder to watch than others.

Standing in the checkout line of a supermarket, we once heard a customer ahead of us speaking to somebody on their brand new iPhone 4. They were excitedly mentioning the purchase of said new device during their conversation.

It had just been released months prior, and the base price was $599.

I didn't really think anything of it until I heard the customer say, "One second, I have to pay real quick..." before reaching into a wallet and pulling out their form of payment.

It was an EBT card.

The customer loudly confirmed with the clerk, "You take SNAP cards, right?"

For those that don't know, SNAP: The Supplemental Nutrition Assistance Program is *intended* to provide assistance purchasing food for needy families.

I'd be curious as to how many people would consider one who could afford a brand new $599 smartphone in 2010 as being, "needy."

Oh, did they qualify because they could only afford the base model instead of the $699 32GB model?

Both Kelly and I were working full-time jobs, had no children, were renting an apartment in a not-very-safe part of town, and could only afford to use our old flip-phones at the time. There's no way one of us could even think about dropping six hundred bucks on a phone.

This person was on food stamps, and had a brand new state of the art smartphone.

How could this be?

Well, all we had to do was look in the mirror.

Could *we* have afforded to go out to restaurants every other day for the last three years?

Of *course* not, we slapped it on credit cards — it was the American way!

In some manner, this person was no different; just like us, they too *needed* to sort out their priorities.

On the other hand, they'd gone one further and were literally exploiting funds from others in order to buy fancy toys.

They could easily have afforded groceries for themselves for *three months* had they chosen to not spend the money on a fancy phone.

They had made some poor decisions.

Kelly and I had absolutely made some too, but we were *paying back* every penny we'd borrowed — exponentially more, with interest of course.

Admittedly, neither scenario is a great example of spending wisely.

While trying to forget that display of exploitation, I saw an even *more* blatant instance a few months later.

I was running a couple errands with my good friend Dustin when we stopped at a small gas station convenience store to each grab a bottle of water.

The inside checkout queue was over 10 parties deep, nearly reaching the back wall.

Everyone in line was irritated — arms crossed, brows furled, and breathing angrily.

Glancing toward the counter, we discovered why people were frustrated.

The front-most customer had decided to do their grocery shopping at this store and had over twenty items being rung up.

There were several individual bags of chips, many tall cans of carbonated energy drinks, a few blue colored mega-sized thirst-quenching beverages, varieties of dried meat snacks, a couple gallons of water, packs of cigarettes and flavored vapes, some disposable lighters, and to polish it off... several *cases* of the fizziest yellowest light beer varieties on the market.

The customer could have easily obtained these items at the supermarket a few blocks away for a fraction of the price.

That was nobody's business but their own.

It was *their money.*

That's not why people were upset.

The clerk had initially rung up all the items under one transaction, and the customer had attempted to pay with an EBT card.

Well, I guess it *wasn't* their money.

Much arguing, voiding, and carefully phrased explanations of what was and was not approved for purchase with the card had been taking place.

After the transaction of EBT-approved foodstuffs was completed, everybody in line now had to wait as the remaining items that had *not* been covered by the card (namely the $100 or more of alcohol and tobacco products) were paid for with a combination of several different credit cards and crumpled bills.

Exclamations of, "Seriously??" and "ARE YOU KIDDIN' ME?!" shouted from the line did no good at all. The customer and clerk alike ignored all outside communications.

After about five minutes in line, the offending transactions were completed, and the rest of the customers were tended to in lightning speed by the *expert** clerk, who apologized to all for the delay.

As Dustin and I returned to the car with our bottled waters, I questioned how it was that somebody could so flagrantly exploit the system like that. They were spending every extra cent they had and charging up debt on beer and smokes, but just *had* to use government benefits to buy food? I couldn't believe the clerk didn't say anything or call them out!

Without a blink, Dustin replied, "They're not allowed to. They're on camera, and can get in big trouble for that... they can be sued for harassment and then some."

He was right. They could have possibly lost their job for speaking up.

I'd known some classmates and friends in my youth with single parents who used government benefit programs legitimately, as they were truly needed.

Those displays of exploitation I witnessed were in a part *taking away* from those honest people in real need, and it was difficult to stand there and watch.

Dustin then mentioned it wasn't the first time he'd seen that sort of thing, and that he had known people (that he no longer spoke with)

*see what I did there?

that regularly did the same.

He said some would even *boast* about their tactics of asking friends or family if they needed any groceries from the store on random visits. Paying for the groceries with their EBT card, they'd then use the cash they were reimbursed with to go out later and party at local bars and clubs.

Later that year, I was hearing out a friend who was a single parent of two, working both a full-time job and another part-time on the side. They had been struggling just to pay rent and raise their children, and had just applied for SNAP and other assistance programs.

They were denied due to having "too high of an income."

It appears that system needs some serious ironing out.

Too many of these displays give off the perception of it rewarding those who aren't putting forth any effort, and penalizing those who are.

Witnessing this series of events had gotten me down a bit and I soon entered into a negative funk for a few months, stewing and loathing about the subject.

To add to my panic and disgust, the impact of the recent real estate crash had people complaining and arguing about the economy on social media more than ever.

Locals I'd known for years were saying they'd have to get an extra job on the side (preferably one where they could get paid under the table) to afford to stay living in the county.

Was that ethical? Was that good for the economy?

I recalled reading an article after high school stating that in California alone, the number of employees being paid under the table accounted for a loss of several billion tax dollars per year.

Well, *I* pay taxes.

I don't cheat the system.

That's not fair, is it?

Others proposed different remedies.

Around that time as so it goes every few years, I saw people once again demanding to raise the minimum wage in California *significantly*, only this time the complaints were in record numbers.

They demanded that the minimum wage be made a "living wage."

What is that, exactly?

Does a "living wage" imply being able to afford your very own apartment, or afford one with roommates?

...*How many* roommates?

Does it imply affording your own car as well?

New or used?

...*How used?*

If not a car, a bike? A bus pass?

Does it suggest only affording groceries to cook at home, or the ability to go out to a restaurant on occasion?

...*How occasionally?*

What about entertainment?

Should people be issued a government stipend for movie theater admission? Theme park tickets? Annual passes to beaches? National parks? Vacation allowance?

For all intents and purposes, a "living wage" is unspecified.

It's a completely subjective term.

There's a difference between people wanting to get their fair share, and those insisting that the world owe them a living.

The ants can only support so many cicadas.

Is that not a strange thing to strive for in the first place?

The *minimum?*

Why are so many aiming for the bottom of the barrel, and demanding what they must be given for a nominal effort?

After a few months of being sucked into this trap of negativity, I had to distance myself from these conversations. Many of them were with people just venting their anger with no intention of taking responsibility for their own actions.

I was closely exposed to such displays after agreeing to help a couple of acquaintances who had asked me for financial advice. They'd either complained they'd just had bad luck and couldn't get ahead, or felt that the system was unfair and completely against them.

In both cases after analyzing their true monthly cost of living versus their spending habits, it was revealed they each were blowing the majority of their incomes on fancy alcohol, expensive cars with payments they couldn't afford, restaurants, a massive cable bill, designer clothing, and a substantial number of credit card payments to cover their excessive spending in the past.

The American Way. Our generations have been taught this is the norm within our culture.

"You're always going to have *some* form of debt..."

In reality, that's another choice. People can choose not to.

Pointing these elements out as the primary culprits of their financial suffering, these people took great offense at my advice that they should create and abide by a modest budget. They stated that it was none of my business how they spent their money, and they wanted no more recommendations from little old me.

They'd *asked me* for assistance — I was only trying to help them.

Clearly, many people *are* perfectly able to improve their financial situations, but have yet to put in the work.

I realized that no matter how depressing it may be witnessing so many others suffer while in reality they have all the power they need to better their lives, in the end I can't do anything for them.

We can't make good decisions for them.

We can't control their actions. (That's a good thing!)

We absolutely can control our own.

Since that realization, Kelly and I have done everything we can to try living responsibly, living within our means, and saving for our future.

It's simple, but not easy.

It's sacrifice, and learning to say "no" to a lot of fun that one can't afford to have.

I regret that I have no resolutions or answers of how to address exploitation, defensive behaviors, and refusal of solicited sound advice.

There are also additional concerns that touch on the concept of freedom versus economic impact, such as the behavior of *some* land owners that comes off as lazy.

There is a well-known once-thriving property of several acres in the Santa Ynez Valley that consisted of about 20 commercial rental units. Over a decade ago, the tenants had started to clear out one by one.

The reason was that many of the units had become neglected, fell into disrepair, and were heavily overpriced.

Over time, 90% of the units went empty for nearly *15 years* as affordable small business space became scarce in the valley.

Progress was stunted. Small businesses waned and struggled. The local economy took quite a hit.

It's not an uncommon pattern, but perhaps more easily noticed in smaller towns.

I never understood the behavior of large commercial property owners allowing even a single unit to go without a tenant for months at a time, much less an entire year!

I know what 12 times nuthin' is…

That property owner's decision to allow a massive commercial center to remain nearly empty for so long was such a shameful and preventable loss of potential income, one wonders what went through their head.

Were they exploiting it as a write-off?

Were they truly just lazy?

Were they so well-off from their other business ventures that they were completely satisfied letting that property rot?

These are all shots in the dark; I don't know anything about their situation.

I also know that no matter how frustrating these occurrences are, I respect their freedom to do with their property as they wish.

That being said, I don't want anybody misquoting me or getting the idea that I feel the upper class are all lazy. I'm saying that I feel it often goes unrealized how much influence they have over the potential for domestic economic growth.

There's a *different* area of town in which another landlord — through thick and thin — has hardly seen an empty unit in decades.

They're known for constantly working with their tenants, at times even temporarily lowering rent during recessions.

The small businesses in those units remain active and successful, and the property owner continues to be paid rent.

Constructive local feedback, and civilized personal communication have power enough to encourage positive change. I don't believe one should be mandated by any government as to what they should be doing with their own land.

Identifying issues within our personal budgets and our economy is easy. Effectively *doing* something about it is an entirely different matter, and usually requires going through some emotional pain.

The longer we wait and the greater these problems become, the greater the financial hardship will be in order to reverse the damage.

In the end, buckling down and exercising discipline leads to both emotional *and* financial growth.

I wish only the best for my home state of California and its residents, and I *hope* I can continue to afford to live here in the future.

V

It's Never Too Late If You Care Enough

My Dad and I had both decided to purchase some air conditioners earlier this year.

We settled on some window units, as opposed to the upright portable models that can ooze heat from their exhaust hoses right back into the room.

Unable to locate any American made products in our area, we decided to buy from an online retailer.

I ordered two large 14,000 BTU Dual Inverter window units from a very popular appliance manufacturer's website.

We also purchased heavy duty mounting brackets, two-by-fours, and plywood.

Upon the units' arrival, we measured and installed all mounting hardware with a perfect fit, powered up one unit, and...

It was defective.

The internal fan had stopped turning after a few seconds. An error code was soon displayed which prompted us to call the manufacturer for support.

Due to thick accents and a language barrier of an outsourced support team, it took several minutes of verbal repetition by *both* parties before understanding that the error code indicated the air conditioner was defective.

It would need to be replaced.

Luckily, the other unit worked fine. We proceeded to install it in my apartment, as my parents said they could wait for the replacement. They had better airflow in their building, and the inside of my own apartment was already getting up to 90°F by early spring.

Two weeks later, the replacement air conditioner arrived. We unboxed it at my parents' place, and decided to test *before* installing it this time.

We plugged it in, powered it on, and...

The fan started rotating!

Alas, only for a few seconds. Visible through the slots on the side of the unit, a small internal part came loose from the top of the case and fell right into the path of the fan blade, physically stopping it from turning further.

My Dad wasn't too impressed.

"That's it — ship it back for a refund, I'm done. I'll shop around more for something locally."

A refund was received upon returning it later that month, but the sting still remained.

Two out of three units had been delivered defective.

Shipping couriers occasionally being less than caring with packages (especially heavy ones) is really nothing new.

Likewise, the grouchy old curmudgeon-like exclamation, "They don't make'm like they used to," is far from exaggeration, and it feels as if it's been getting worse.

Looking at my order history from online retailers, I realized I'd attempted to purchase no less than 10 appliances in the last two years for the kitchen or office. Including those two AC units, I've ended up returning six of those items for being defective upon arrival.

It's getting more difficult to find American made products, which means less support for our domestic economy and local jobs. It also puts one at the mercy of potentially waiting *days* for a response from a customer service department that operates strictly through email. To twist the knife, the expectations set are less than frequently met.

"Buying American" is also no longer as transparent.

A wristwatch might have a craftily worded label on the box such as, "Made With American Materials" or "Assembled In America," only for one to find that though the leather strap was made in America, the watch itself was made in China, or sourced with foreign materials.

When shopping for clothing, one could easily be under the impression that an American designer brand that offers designs of palm trees and island motifs on their $140 shirts might perhaps have them made in Hawai'i... only to find out they too are made in China.

That goes for a large amount of clothing sold in America, and some of these companies aren't exactly forthcoming about their specific factory locations or material sources.

Let me make one thing abundantly clear: I have nothing against the Chinese people, and I'm absolutely not against purchasing products outside of one's country, provided they're ethically made.

I also don't conduct self-righteous social media witch-hunts to berate people based on where they choose to shop. Regardless, I sleep a little better at night knowing *I'm* trying not to support companies that exercise immoral business practices.

This is much easier said than done, and nobody's perfect.

China usually gets the worst publicity regarding this matter due to the exploitation involving labor camps such as those in Xinjiang. Just do a little reading about the treatment of the Uyghurs in China. They're literally traded as slaves in labor camps, and mistreated to the point of what several investigating governments have defined as torture.

The Media often refers to it as "forced labor," but it's blatant slavery — it should be called out for what it is.

These practices are greatly affected by people from many countries who have no issue with this exploitation.

This includes the United States of America.

I have a local friend who creates and sells her very own hand-made wooden signs, crafts, and intricately decorated greeting cards.

She was approached by an impressed American customer who introduced themselves as a representative of a larger company. *They* could help her expand her business through their services based in China to mass produce her creations.

She turned them down, wanting nothing to do with it.

These representatives have been fishing around with their craft more persistently in recent decades, and larger companies have long been biting.

The action of American businesses outsourcing materials and labor makes for quite the negative statement.

It says, "I'd rather send money outside the country for cheaper materials and labor in order to line my pockets *faster* instead of creating and supporting jobs here domestically."

Not respectable, and not good for the economy.

Anybody who's called customer service or tech support knows that it's rare to have a human initially answer the phone anymore, much less somebody who isn't difficult to understand.

Outsourcing has been destroying customer service, and violating accountability.

I've seen it happening gradually for decades.

Quality service has been fizzling for years as large corporations continue to skimp on properly trained, educated employees right here in our own country.

One major technology company was even berated very recently by a celebrity on national television for knowingly utilizing factories that exercise despicable practices.

Though some jeered at the candor of the harsh call-out, further awareness had been raised of foreign child labor, and of such poor working conditions in some Chinese factories that "suicide nets" are utilized to decrease the number of employees jumping out the windows.

Many companies operating with poor labor practices in China are actually American-owned.

China has long taken this bad rap, but don't believe for a moment that they're a purely sinister country enabling evil slave owners.

That would be a completely unfair, ignorant, and foolish delusion.

After all, when was the last time *you* were pleased with, and felt represented by every decision of your local government or domestic corporations?

Your Mayor?

Your State Governor?

Your Congress?

...Your President?

Would you wish for citizens of other countries to judge *you* based on the actions of any domestic government or company's politics?

Is that a fair assessment?

The actions of governments or corporations should never be held as a personal representation of individual citizens. That's a fantastic method of breeding bigotry, and encouraging xenophobia.

No honor comes from it.

Some are quick to try playing the racist card when one complains about foreign outsourcing, but there is nothing racist about the irritation of being unable to understand the words coming out of a human's mouth when calling for help with a product that was purchased locally.

Outsourcing happens domestically as well, and it's no picnic.

I once worked for an American company that outsourced the majority of its tech support department to an out-of-state temp agency.

They paid pennies above minimum wage.

Though *every one* of those employees were born and raised Americans, they'd had such nominal technical experience that some didn't know how to locate the Control Panel in Windows, or what a Desktop or Registry was.

That's simply poor business practice. You can't efficiently resolve problems when wrestling a communication breakdown, or speaking to an under-qualified staff.

Several companies have gone out of their way to reveal that respectable factory conditions in China are absolutely a reality, and on the rise. Just enter a web query looking for, "ethical companies in China," and you'll find many.

At the risk of repeating myself, I'm not encouraging anybody to boycott any and all products or services from countries outside their own. There's a very thick line between pride in one's country, and exercising prejudice.

I'd be ecstatic to see one brand of cell phone, a laptop, any electronic device, a computer component, or appliance from a factory where its employees aren't exploited, abused, or underpaid. The origin of country doesn't matter to me as much as the end product being of ethical, respectable quality.

This is a very possible change, and I'm doing what I can one step at a time.

It continues to prove difficult.

I've been trying for years to support my domestic economy by prioritizing local products and services, but after going through that irritating ordeal with defective air conditioners, I realized I could try even harder.

That experience resulted in spending nearly four hours in a single night searching the web for 100% ethically produced, American made and sourced wares, only to come up with frustrating results:

Very few were found, and for the most part were extremely expensive:

- Decorative paper notes priced at $30 for a small pad.
- Watches manufactured in the USA with imported Swiss parts were $300. Those with 100% domestically sourced parts were well over $1,000.
- Hiking boots for no less than $270.
- Denim pants for $98, sweat pants for $64.
- A Single T shirt could not be found under $30.
- Boxer shorts for $20. (For one pair!)

That's apparently what 100% domestic products cost nowadays.

I picture the hackneyed, stereotyped image throughout our country's history of a flag-waving patriot shouting out, "America!" with pride in their hearts and voices.

What *does* America make today? What do we create ourselves anymore?

Surely not any motor vehicles with our own parts...

Are Americans willing to pay what it costs for clothing, watches, paper, furniture, and other items to bring our economy back up from where it is?

(Perhaps nobody's "buying American" anymore because so little is available to buy *affordably*.)

In the 1980s, one parent's full-time job would often make enough money to allow the other to raise two children at home.

In many cities today, two adults have to work full time to struggle paying rent *without* children.

Our economy is in the toilet, and repeatedly raising the minimum wage hasn't seemed to help very much in the long run, has it?

Not at all.

Our national debt has skyrocketed in the last 40 years and continues to increase sharply with each presidency, while zealous party loyalists can do naught but ping-pong the blame of said rising debt on the *opposing* party's prior officeholders.

Clearly, blaming presidents for single-handedly causing grief hasn't worked.

At all.

To quote Robert Francis Goldthwait from back in the late 1980s, "Blaming Ronald Reagan for the way things are today is kinda like blaming Ronald McDonald when you get a bad cheeseburger — neither of'm run the company, folks!"

Despite this embarrassing behavior of the masses, sooner or later the realization may dawn on an individual:

Every one of us makes up "the masses" and has the power to incite positive change.

It's never too late to turn things around.

To work my way toward positive motivation, here are some practices I've tried to adopt whenever possible:

First and foremost, I try to shop local.

My town has a farmers market only once a week, but several farms have their own stands on location from which they sell their produce daily. It's priced lower than that of grocery stores, and is usually much fresher. We also have a few local butcher shops that sell humanely raised quality meats.

It's quite possible that depending on where you live, your nearest local farm stand is closer than you think. Once you taste same-day fresh lettuce leaves, you'll never want to buy a head of lettuce in a supermarket again, either.

It's life-changing, and perhaps even a little maddening when you start to wonder *how old* those lettuce heads on the grocery store shelf really are.

We don't have a major electronics or appliance outlet in the Santa Ynez Valley, nor a large clothing store.

Much of our locally sold attire is either upscale, or casual wear aimed at tourists.

When shopping local isn't an option, our next choices are to drive out of town for a short road trip, or shop online.

I have located several affordable products that are made domestically and ethically, and though the list of items within my budget is short, I'm always looking for more:

Socks. **Fitsok** is a family-owned company founded in 2008 out of North Carolina. They offer many styles of socks currently at the price of $20 for three pairs, and they had a 40% off sale when I stocked up a few months ago. They're comfy and durable — far more so than the mass produced outlet brands I'd previously been purchasing. I'll never go back.

Pens. People like a good pen that fits in their hand and works well every time. **Fisher Space Pen Company** of Boulder City, Nevada has hundreds of models of pens for purchase on their website, and their pressurized cartridge refills are legendary. If you don't want to drop $70 on an original Astronaut Space Pen, they offer plenty others starting at just $6. I bought a mid-range model for a friend as a birthday gift earlier this year, and the company engraved it at no extra charge. It's gorgeous, and has a lifetime guarantee against defects.

Hygiene Products. Though they were purchased by Proctor & Gamble in late 2017, **Native** still offers bar soap, shower gel, deodorant, toothpaste, and sunscreen, all of which are made in the USA without harmful ingredients.

Flashlights. When the power goes out, you want a reliable light source. From key chain miniatures to larger sizes worthy of a camp site, **Maglite** still manufactures their durable products in the United States.

Lighters. The amount of money wasted on disposable lighters is huge. You can still buy a classic **Zippo** lighter made in the USA with a lifetime warranty against defects starting under $20. They're most always on sale at many retailers for even less, too.

Cookware. Not every piece of **Lodge Cast Iron Cookware** is made in the USA (specifically, their enamel products are made in China *overseen by an American-owned third-party inspection company*), but their classic seasoned cast iron products are made in Tennessee. Subjectively, I personally chose to remove the seasoning with a powerful sander, and then seasoned it traditionally myself. I personally feel it performs better.*

Blenders. **Blendtec** and **Vitamix** blenders are both made in America. It is unclear to me if 100% of their parts are domestically sourced, but these were the best I could locate when shopping around. A friend of mine ended up going with the Vitamix, and I ended up choosing a Blendtec as it happened to be on a great sale. I use it just about every day, and it's hands down the highest quality kitchen appliance I've ever owned. In turn, my friend raves about the quality of the Vitamix equally.

---

*Many thanks to Cowboy Cook Mr. Kent Rollins of Hollis, Oklahoma for this outstanding advice.

It's not the longest list, but it's a start. Not having to funnel most of our paychecks into credit card and loan payments anymore has allowed Kelly and me to get away from buying cheaply made products.

We don't make any impulse buys these days either, as we like to research brand names and study product performance reviews to get better bang for our buck.

It's working. Our purchased products are lasting well, and we're spending less in the long run.

Perhaps if enough people invest in products that were manufactured with high quality standards and ethical business practices, this list may grow sooner rather than later.

I'm doing the best that I can.

I'll continue to try buying local, and if I can't find what I'm after, I will *gladly* seek out and support ethically made foreign goods and products to promote them as well.

I wouldn't expect any different from other people in their own countries.

vi

How We Did It

Kelly and I realized the first step to a healthy financial future was to get rid of our $85,000 debt.

College made up about half of that, credit cards the rest.

Why so much credit card debt? Well, ya see...

My poor decision to keep holding on to a decrepit car long past its prime had resulted in thousands of dollars in repairs, time and again.

Beyond that, spending every penny leftover after our cost of living (and then some) on entertainment and luxuries *very easily* racked up tens of thousands of dollars on credit cards.

We're not alone — remember that average personal debt of $56,000? It's how it's done!

Not proud of that.

The temptations are different for everybody. Some can't resist going to the movies several times a week. Many go to live shows and concerts. Others trade in for new cars and the latest appliances every year, but we've got a different vice:

We *love* going to restaurants.

Back in 2008, we'd hit a rough patch of depression after the country suffered the real estate crash and a dip in the job market. We were having a terrible experience living in an area with infamously gloomy weather, and we had a difficult time dealing with all that.

To cope, we went out to eat. Often.

Very often.

I'm talking up to five nights a week at full service restaurants, and sometimes twice a day on weekends.

Restaurants are *luxurious!* You don't have to cook or clean, and if one doesn't have much *personal* experience in their own kitchen, the food is usually much more creative than at home!

It's also about 10 times the price.

It's *worth the money* in our opinion.

We love to support local restaurants!

We just can't afford to do so every single meal.

That's us. That's our weakness. It may be the same for others, it may not. One needs only to assess their spending habits, and look at the bottom line.

"What did I spend this month beyond the necessary cost of living?"

First, I suppose one has to know what the cost of living should be.

That's a subjective question. *We* decided to make a budget based on how much money we wanted to save in order to retire by age 67.

We agreed on a number, and based on the incomes of our current career jobs, created a budget that would help us both get out of debt and start catching up on saving and investing for our retirement.

Our Chosen Budget:

Category	% of Income
Housing & Utilities	25
Transportation	10
Food	10-15
Health Insurance	10
Personal (Misc, Hygiene)	5
Household	5
Clothing	5
Incidentals	5
Saving & Investing/Debt	10-15+
Entertainment	5
Charity	5+

This is our budget. Our goal. Our guideline.

Some categories are easier to abide by than others. I'll cover each category very briefly, and give a few tips that have helped us keep things in check.

Housing & Utilities

This one's easy. Rent is the same price every month.

The amount of our water bill is consistent as we each take one shower daily, plan efficient loads of laundry, and wash dishes by hand.

To save on electricity, we wear extra layers of clothes and blankets in the winter, and set the AC to 78°F in the summer.

Our shared cell phone plan has a nominal amount of data that rolls over, and we keep our web browsing to a minimum when not connected to Wi-Fi. I'm personally accustomed to looking at maps and getting directions to my destinations *before* I leave home, so I won't be seen draining very much data via GPS.

I'm by no means an obsessive planner, but I like knowing where I'm driving before I get into a vehicle. Speaking of...

Transportation

We're very fortunate to live in a small town where desired gas stations, grocery stores, and farms are all within a five mile range.

My chiropractor is 35 miles away, and I go twice a month. We usually plan any other "big city" shopping and errands for those days too, minimizing out-of-town driving and saving us money.

When I lived in San Diego, I carpooled often with co-workers, and we rotated drivers for courtesy.

If I wasn't lucky enough to live nearby any coworkers, I'd probably opt for public transportation. I *personally* wouldn't feel comfortable using a ridesharing service.

As for keeping our auto insurance affordable, Kelly and I both exercise patience and focus while driving, removing ego from the equation as to avoid poor decisions. We like to drive using our wits rather than our emotions; the road has no room for spite.

(Don't drive angry.)

We've no tickets *or* accidents on our records.

Finally, we reevaluate our coverage twice a year to adjust for the depreciation of our vehicle.

Review the rules of the road, don't break them, avoid unnecessary trips, and don't insure your vehicle above its worth. That's our approach.

Food

This is where things get interesting.

It's easy to stay within our limit, provided we... *shop smart*.

That means both keeping an eye out for sales, but also what we buy.

Anytime food is involved, time is money. The smallest amount of meal prep can make quite a difference when striving to meet one's budget.

Our habit is to buy as little precooked or prepared food as possible. I'm not referring to frozen boxed meals or hot counter foods alone, but single ingredients as well.

Take a can of black beans, for instance. Even on sale, we're talking about $1.50 per can.

After removing the lid and draining the fluid, that's a cup and a half of beans you're left with. For the same price, you can buy an entire pound of dry beans from the bulk section. That'll make you about *seven cups* once cooked.

It's easy: Just rinse, add to a pot with plenty of water, season as desired, cover, and do whatever you like as it simmers for two hours. You can even cut that cooking time drastically if you soak the beans overnight.

Buy purchasing one pound in dry bulk, you've spent $1.50 instead of the $10.50 it would have cost for the same amount in cans.

That's 85% less.

The savings are similar with grains, legumes, nuts, and just about *anything* you can find in the dry bulk section.

With nominal cooking practice, they'll also taste exponentially better than their canned counterparts.

We prefer fresh protein, too. We try to buy all of our pastured and/or kosher quality meats fresh and raw from local stores who support nearby farms. Occasionally, we'll even go right to the source and purchase from local butchers.

As mentioned before, fruits and veggies are exponentially fresher from farms than in the grocery store, but the same habit applies: If we don't make it to the farmers market, we buy whole foods in the produce section, and cut into them only when we're ready to eat.

There's a balance to be found when purchasing in larger quantities to save money by gauging how much food you can keep in your kitchen before it spoils. Every household will be different depending on the number of people, their level of activity, and how often they eat at home versus dining out.

One strict motto is that if you're in debt and trying to pay it off, it's best to abstain from eating out at restaurants entirely.

That may be optimal, but we felt that was a bit *too* strict for us. We ended up limiting ourselves to affordable restaurants just a couple times a month, as having an occasional date night feeds the soul and serves our relationship well.

Health Insurance

This one's been a sore subject for us ever since the Affordable Care Act was passed because it has caused us much pain — both financially and physically. I'll try to summarize quickly without dwelling on it.

Before the ACA, Kelly and I had a basic individual plan that covered us both for a mere $120 per month. We'd opted for a very high deductible to save on monthly premiums, but we still had a $35 co-pay for urgent care, preventative care, chiropractic care, and discounted generic prescriptions.

Once the new law was passed in 2010, our plan was immediately invalidated, and the cheapest plan available in California (the "Covered California" Bronze plan) was $845 per month.

That rate briefly dipped below $800 in 2020, then rose again to $830 in mid summer of 2021.

Since we can't afford a healthcare plan until either the system gets ironed out or I find a new employer offering an affordable group plan, we're setting aside 10% of our income for health care emergencies at the moment.

It's all we can afford to do.

We take great care of ourselves, get plenty of sleep, and practice proper nutrition and exercise as to minimize the likelihood of a medical emergency.

Still, without a health insurance plan at the moment, a broken limb or even minor surgery would likely bankrupt us.

Personal, Household, Clothing, and Incidentals

We tried to track these categories monthly, and realized it isn't so easy to spend a consistent dollar amount since we don't buy household cleaner, toothpaste, closet hangers, ant traps, or even clothing every single month.

No items in these categories should be breaking the bank, but we've established some methods to keep the spending even lower:

Toiletries, kitchenware, clothes, and cleaning products are much cheaper when avoiding expensive designer brands and keeping an eye out for sales on classics.

We try not to wait to let work clothes, denims, or shoes go until they're completely thrashed, at which point we may be forced to pay full retail price when we need something at a moment's notice.

We keep wish lists of all items in these categories because we know we're going to need them, and if it so happens we stock up on something within reason for a deal, they're *going* to get used in the near future.

Simple Green All-Purpose Cleaner is a long-time personal favorite. We buy the classic gallon size of the concentrate, as it lasts for years and is one of the few products we've found that's both non-toxic and actually cleans well. Though some don't love the scent of it, we really don't mind it once it's been diluted in a spray bottle.

We've been sticking to Native brand products this year due to their great prices, free shipping in the USA without a minimum order, and lack of harmful ingredients.

Quality, ethically made clothing is expensive, and these are the items we've found require the most diligence in looking out for deals. Personally, I usually keep one pair of denim pants that I can beat up and wear often around the apartment, saving nicer pairs for going out. That goes the same for shirts.

Taking care and observing washing instructions for delicates goes a long way, too.

It's not rocket science: Buy quality products and treat them well, and they'll prove far more resilient versus buying cheaply made brands, saving you big money in the long run.

Our Debt Payoff

Once we decided to take up arms against our debt, the first thing we did was cut all unnecessary spending after our cost of living.

We both accepted overtime whenever it was offered.

I wore torn, stained jeans while working at home.

We canceled all unnecessary monthly recurring items like video game subscriptions, magazines, and any extra Cable TV packages. We even decreased our home internet speed.

We kept restaurants to only a couple outings a month. That was exceedingly difficult for us.

We stopped buying processed foods, desserts, alcohol, and started buying whole food items while increasing our kitchen skills using books and online resources.

We sold our second vehicle at the time.

We bought generic brand toiletries, stopped going out to movies, and put weekend vacations on hold — which was really just going to restaurants in other towns, anyway.

(Jim Gaffigan was right.)

This helped us kick-start our ability to come in under budget, as well as actually stop racking up debt.

A $1,000 backup fund was then established within our checking account. We never spent below that balance; it was for emergencies only.

Finally, we used what has been referred to as the "avalanche" method, popularly held as a most efficient way to pay down debt:

We'd gather up the bills every month, and determine which creditor was costing us the highest monthly dollar amount in interest at that moment.

(If you have an aversion to doing the math, there are many calculators online to enter the balance and APR of all your debts to show which one is leeching the most interest.)

We'd pay the minimum on all bills, and then *slam* every extra penny we had on the account guzzling the most interest.

Rinse and repeat until debt is paid off.

Another popular plan is the "snowball" method:

This involves paying off the debts with the lowest balance first, resulting in the emotional gratification of seeing one of your credit cards or loans to be quickly paid off and closed. This is a benefit to those who are discouraged and *feel* like they're not making any progress.

Our emotions can control our behaviors, and although the avalanche method will pay off your debt faster and with less interest lost, sometimes we may need a little boost of confidence by seeing a credit card with a smaller balance disappear.

We did switch to the snowball method a couple times when we yearned for that gratification, but stuck mainly to the avalanche.

The choice is yours, and both methods are functional and respectable.

After our debts were paid off, we removed the word "Debt" from our budget, and began to save and invest.

Saving & Investing

My first job at 16 years old paid minimum wage, which was $4.25 per hour at the time. My last raise at age 40 put me over the $30 per hour mark.

Aside from establishing a 401k with my latest employer in 2004, I've only just begun properly investing a few years ago.

I'm kicking myself for waiting so long to start.

Here's a little set of numbers to encourage people to prevent regret by starting to invest at a young age:

Today (9-10-21), if a couple at age 21 were to both start working full-time minimum wage jobs in California and contribute only 10% of their paychecks after tax every month to a mutual fund with a 7% return compiled annually, that investment will have grown to over 1.5 million dollars by age 67.

That's also an unrealistically *low* number, as it anticipates they'll forever shoot for the bottom, never get a promotion, and minimum wage will never increase.

A great variety of mutual funds exist that have had a 30 year history or longer of showing well over 7%... some over 10%!

Which of these sounds like a wiser investment to *prioritize:* buying a house, or turning $200,000 of contributions into over 1.5 million dollars by retirement?

401k, IRA, Roth IRA, Mutual Funds, and other investment options all have different advantages, risks, and tax rules. It's absolutely worth your time to give a call to a respected local financial service professional to discuss your options, then decide for yourself what works best for you.

Remember that the above example was shown by contributing just 10% of a *minimum wage* income; just imagine if one applies themselves to achieve a great paying job and contributes 15%!

As a safety net before we started investing, *we* established a savings account to grow our backup fund large enough to cover six months worth of living expenses in case of an emergency.

Though I *had* established that 401k with my employer back in 2004, I'd only ever contributed 5%. I'd even stopped contributing to it for a few years in order to more quickly pay down our debt, so it was off to a lousy start.

To make things worse, the investment company my employer had selected did a terrible job, and I rarely received more than a 4% return.

Scandalous.

A couple of years ago, I rolled it over to an IRA where I can control which funds are invested in, and I'm now seeing returns of well over 8%.

Since paying off our debt, we've been pinching every single penny to come in under budget on every category possible.

This includes *housing,* by living in an old beat-up one bedroom apartment with holes in the floor and 30 year old poorly functioning appliances.

Our mantra: *"Cheap rent... Cheap rent... Cheap rent..."*

<u>Entertainment</u>

Ah, we've finally arrived.

The main distraction.

It was for *us*, anyway.

In 2011, we had still been spending almost half our income on entertainment. I was 31 years old.

We successfully put a choke-hold on our absurd restaurant spending, and once we established a four-year payoff plan, we paid off our debt...

In nine years.

We, uh... deviated from the plan often.

It was difficult to break our spending habits; self-discipline has never been an easy skill to develop.

I've long observed that pain is a harsh yet fair teacher. Once Kelly and I experienced enough pain, we began associating our carelessly excessive spending with long-term pain as opposed to the short-term pleasure it would provide.

It was a bumpy and brutal trek, but over time our self-discipline grew stronger. We're now quickly catching up on our retirement balance by contributing above and beyond, every chance we get.

To save money while still having *fun*, we've found great success with the following:

- **Books:** Kelly and I enjoy reading. There are multiple free online apps that allow you to check out e-books and audiobooks without spending a dime. Just like when searching for a physical book at public libraries (which we also frequent), you may have to add a few titles to a waiting list if they're in high demand.
- **The Outdoors:** Exercise is a great way for me to get out of the house, since I've worked remotely for nearly 20 years. Wouldn't ya know it, it also keeps the body in shape.
- **Media:** We take advantage of premium streaming services for a fraction of the price of a Cable TV plan. As for music, we occasionally use a free streaming service while complaining frequently about the incessantly annoying commercials.
- **Video Games:** I rarely pay full price for a brand new title; I purchase most of my games *used* for far less than 50% under retail price. Additionally, there are several digital game distribution platforms that offer excellent sales, and some even give a game or two away every week just for registering and installing their desktop client on your computer! Taking advantage of this for the last couple of years, I've amassed well over 200 PC game titles for free, many of them indicating a $50 retail value. Truth be told however, when a major first party franchise title from Nintendo comes along, I'm *going* to be throwing down full price on day one. *Metroid Dread* releases next month, and I've already saved and set aside the money.
- **Restaurants:** Now that we're debt-free, restaurant visits are kept at one per week. We try to keep ordering alcoholic beverages at a minimum, as just ordering *two* can potentially double the price of a meal.

Charity

It's a reality: When you're in debt, you can't afford to give much to charity. We chose to get out of debt first, *then* start investing, *then* were able to start giving generously. We don't usually donate directly to organizations, as we prefer to give privately, anonymously, or participate in local fundraisers or events to help those in need. Everybody should make their own decision about whether or not and how much they choose to give to charity, and shaming should never enter the equation.

When we were scrimping to pay off our debt, we tried to keep our entertainment as low as possible — even 1% some months. Getting sucked into a good trilogy of books, a TV series, or an immersive role playing game is a great way to relax and enjoy life without spending very much money.

Since we started investing, we've kept many of those good habits that were picked up. When shopping for appliances and electronic devices, I first look for refurbished models with certified warranties. We still seek out used media, and usually cook at home six days a week.

Kitchen skills are always a work in progress. Some meals were disastrous for the first couple of days months, and we're both still learning.

Cooking is a big deal, and it's also a big payoff.

We've learned our personal preferences for affordable recreation, and continue to be frugal as we make our way toward stronger financial stability.

I'm confident others can too.

Though the following is the greatest advice I can give for a sound financial future, I'm afraid it isn't any different than what many have stated in the past until they're blue in the face:

Plan ahead, stick to a smart budget, and avoid personal debt *at all costs.*

I'd have benefited exponentially more if I'd been wiser 23 years ago, but I'm glad we've got a handle on things as they are, rather than even later.

It is never *too soon* to start.

4

Don't Never Stop Learning

It's Worth It

I'm still occasionally learning little tricks to refine cooking scrambled eggs at age 41. Mine are the fluffiest and most flavorful I've ever tasted.

I have a friend who's a master of growing chile peppers, and I'll be planting some this spring to gain some experience for myself.

I'm still familiar with the general concepts of programming (having taught myself a great deal of Atari BASIC in my youth), but I don't have any experience coding in current-day computer languages like Python, or that legendary champion of the gaming industry, C++.

I'm tempted to start dabbling.

Our pummeled economy saw me swept aside by the last wave of layoffs in May of 2020 after a loyal 17 years with my most recent employer.

It's surreal, having worked full time since age 17 and never having been unemployed until now.

It seems pandemics will have that effect.

My efforts to land a decent paying remote job in the technical industry continue, as the available positions are a bit to be desired.

Postings are predominantly for front line tech support, paying a mere dollar above minimum wage.

Others are starting around $40k per year with larger companies that have quite the illogical fixation on Bachelor's degrees as a non-negotiable requirement.

As I've been making $65k per year *without* a college degree, one can understand if I don't exactly jump to the nearest university for eight semesters so that I may earn 30% less than my worth.

Honestly, for any company operating in this year of 2021 demanding that California citizens invest tens of thousands of dollars *and* four years of their time to be considered for a job that's offering less than $20 per hour, I would question if their CEO were of sound mind.

I can't *believe* companies are still playing this game.

This habit of theirs posed a challenge decades ago, and still does.

It doesn't matter that I've coached teams of front line, second level, and third level agents for years.

It doesn't matter that I've helped create and manage multiple Knowledge Bases from scratch.

It doesn't matter that I have nearly 25 years experience in hardware and software support, and over a decade of technical writing with certifications to boot...

Since I don't have a college degree, many employers won't even take the time to interview me.

The good news is that there are still many who will, albeit few and far between at the moment — the economy is simply still recovering with the majority of states still on lockdown.

With a little patience and reflection, it's very easy to turn bitterness and indignation into both humor and fuel for personal growth.

This is why I've turned to writing books in the interim; it's only improved my writing proficiency on both creative and technical levels.

Additionally, not having the extra cash to throw at an illustrator or editor has resulted in two new skills being added to my repertoire.

It's been a blast, but it's not realistic as an indie author just starting out to instantly expect to earn a decent living.

For every hardcover I sell online or through special order, I hardly make a dollar.

Though that's a much better deal than what most musicians earn per album sale, at this rate I'd still need to sell over 100,000 books a year to meet the income of my last full-time job. Therefore as I continue writing, I'm simultaneously hunting daily for another position to help make ends meet.

This is why I'm now leaning toward pursuing a reputable programming certification to broaden my career scope a bit.

College is just one method of continuing one's education after graduating high school. It has never served as proof that an applicant has acquired the necessary knowledge or skills to serve a position well.

After all, a great majority of city colleges and universities alike require students to maintain only a 2.0 GPA... *merely a C average,* to obtain a degree.

One need only put forth a perfunctory effort.

My former employer exercised a very fair pay system. It wasn't based on one's acquired degrees or certifications (those only assisted in getting you an interview), but was determined by your performance statistics.

I was often proudly among the top 10% of performers in my department. I brought passion to my work, and was always doing what I could do to self-educate and refine my troubleshooting methods on my own time.

Of these top performers, less than half had college degrees. As for the *rest* of the department, about a third of them had disclosed that they'd earned one as well.

Although I consider one's educational experience to be somewhat personal information, it was typically an open topic among many in the department. This was because those *with* degrees often voiced claims of being treated unfairly for not being promoted before those *without* one.

Over time, it ended up resembling a smear campaign led by the indignant, with many of them resorting to throwing others under the bus to try getting ahead.

Clearly, a college degree does *not* necessarily reflect an acquired level of maturity.

Back then, there was a very popular private university in San Diego that was among the most affordable of its kind, and many of the aforementioned grumblers boasted of their attendance.

In truth, this university had a reputation as being somewhat less than fantastic.

Much like buying a house, going to college purely for the sake of doing so is *never* a "sure investment."

It's a tool, and like every tool is only as useful as the one who wields it.

One should also take care in selecting the *proper* tool for the job at hand.

Several of these college graduates were some of the lowest performers in the department. They showed little interest in their tech support position, had short tempers, poor customer service skills, lack of basic operating system knowledge, and the inability to type by touch.

Some had been working there for several years, and still ranked as first level support technicians.

At first, I was flabbergasted how this could be, when *they had a college education.*

Talking with the most successful employees who had obtained degrees, they always tried their best to ignore the self-righteous ones while frequently dropping the line, "You get out of college what you put into it."

That phrase has still stuck with me.

In all my years of speaking with coworkers who were college graduates, none have told me they were asked to show proof of where they'd obtained their degree *or* disclose their GPA to any employers. Many explained they were personally gauged like the rest of us — by "talking shop" during the interview process as for managers to feel out perceived levels of expertise.

College absolutely has the potential to be an excellent tool.

If one is freshly out of high school and has earned grants and scholarships galore, that's a fantastic opportunity. It would be shameful to forfeit such hard-earned benefits.

If for some reason the very real elements of location, timing, family affairs, life events, or last but not least — your budget — prevents college from becoming a reality at any given time, a certification program might work as a practical alternative.

While degrees provide a more general education that often prepares one for a particular position in a desired career path, certifications are very focused on specific skills related to a field.

As I've worked my way up through the tech support industry using my high school education and passionate determination in a field I love, I've ended up obtaining something priceless:

Experience.

This has proven to be as valuable, or to some employers more so than that of an applicant with a college degree and *no* experience.

I've paid cash along the way for many classes in certification programs, successfully avoiding debt yet still furthering my education.

I've gone out of my way to self-educate by reading many of the same books and manuals used in college courses throughout my career.

If I were to drop everything and pursue a degree at this point, I'd be up against a spectacularly boring first few years.

I could even argue that it would literally be a waste of my time, and I'd be largely catering to the "game" that many companies are playing: over-glorification of "The Degree" as the end-all mic drop.

My goal has been to be rather selective with my certification paths chosen, aiming to acquire credits that may later also qualify toward degree credits.

It just takes a little planning, and selecting one's educational institution and courses wisely.

A fine example is the private university I mentioned earlier — it permanently closed a few years ago. I can't imagine the frustration of having started a *proprietary* certification or degree program there that wasn't transferable to other universities.

This happens from time to time, and it's a raw deal.

Tribulations and risks aside, the idea of furthering one's education should *never* be balked at, whether it's college, certifications, a trade apprenticeship, reading another book, or even starting with an entry-level position.

Immersing myself in on-the-job training to obtain new skills and pull in money while paying cash for certifications has served me quite well.

Just like college, you get out of a job what you put into it, too.

It's Not Worth It

Chances are high that none of your future employers are going to care about your college mascot or colors. They likely won't care how many generations of your family have attended the same university, and as mentioned before may not even *ask* where you attended.

They'll only care how well you perform your job.

Some of the most painful comments I've heard from those who attended college was their professing long after graduation to have chosen a major they didn't desire in order to appease their parents.

Some even disclosed they'd been guilt-tripped into pursuing a certain career based on the fact that their parents were paying for their tuition in full — of which they were frequently reminded.

I have no respect for this act of emotional extortion.

Furthering one's education should be a positive experience; learning can be a *thrilling* adventure.

As the presence of substantial college debt being perceived as normalcy is finally a growing concern, many have come to realize how affordable a four-year degree can be when planning for it wisely.

Completing as many credits as possible at a city college before transferring to a four-year university can very realistically get you some Bachelor's degrees for less than $30,000 — the price of a mid size sedan.

Though it's possible you may need to take night classes while holding a full-time job and sharing rent with family or roommates, you'll be simultaneously *gaining experience in your field,* even if starting at an entry level job pertinent to your career path.

Studying textbooks alone may not prepare all of us for the task at hand. My favorite and most effective courses taken were those in which the professor exercised a triad of teaching methods: auditory, visual, and kinesthetic.

They spoke, demonstrated, and then had *us* perform the activity in question as to increase retention of each lesson's material.

I've found some on-the-job training to be equally efficient.

Respectable companies may even be extra quick to hire you if you express intent to further your education while under their employ, and many offer assistance programs to reimburse up to a limited amount per year for any classes related to a degree or certification in your field.

That's quite a benefit.

Taking on loans even for smaller amounts with low interest rates can still end in grief.

Banks can, and do go bankrupt.

This has on occasion resulted in students who have been approved for another semester to end up receiving a certain life-changing phone call from a less than pleased university administration office.

In so many words:

"So, uh... where's our money? Your bank still hasn't sent a check and hasn't returned our phone calls..."

This happened years ago to somebody I know, and they hadn't a clue their once respected bank had disappeared off the face of the planet, until several days *past* the point of no return.

Per university policy, it was too late to drop out and be reimbursed any tuition for the remainder of the semester, owing it in full.

They were also left without funds to pay for housing.

By that point, existing banks were only accepting loan applications for the *following* semesters.

They'd been fleeced.

Criminal behavior, that — by the bank and university alike.

Though that's not a common occurrence, it's one of many complications that could arise from taking on any debt.

Education is no different than any other category in one's budget.

Widespread financial woes involving schooling have become such a presence, politicians have often pandered with promises of college loan forgiveness which has given rise to social unrest and greater political divides.

Many took offense to learn their tax dollars might be going toward someone's acquired education from an expensive university all because the student(s) decided against a more affordable option.

Those who had responsibly paid off their loans (as was promised when the loan agreement was signed...) argued the unfair reality that it wasn't possible to return one's education for a refund.

Student loans are not devoid of risk, and everybody has to make their own decisions of how to further their education responsibly.

Some of them aren't so simple. Pressures and smarmy sales tactics are just as prevalent in the field of education as it is at used car lots, and to an extent, *those establishments should be held responsible.*

One thing's for sure: Being hit in the pocketbook with exploitation hurts everybody.

"Buy now, pay later" is far from resembling the most respectable and healthy financial advice.

"Learn now, pay later" isn't much better.

5

The Selling of Science and an Unstable Pyramid

Lies and Lousy Science

From fifth grade all the way through the end of high school, I was provided with a rather terrible education in nutrition.

The legendary food pyramid along with several accompanying worksheets had drilled a pant-load of falsehoods into my young head:

Pant-load of Falsehoods

- You should always take a daily multivitamin to ensure your body is getting everything it needs.
- The most important food group you should be putting 6-11 servings of down your throat every day is carbohydrates, especially fortified processed name brand cereals and slices of bread. They're healthy because they're made of grain, fortified with superior synthetic nutrients, and are fat-free. (Specific brand names of cereals *were* in fact promoted in the classroom!)
- Foods won't make you gain weight if the nutrition facts indicate the product contains little or no fat.
- Eating too many calories from fat is what causes you to become overweight. Treat oils and fats sparingly, as you would desserts.
- You don't need much protein to stay in shape. A small amount daily will do.
- Be sure to eat a serving of fruits and vegetables with every meal. Frozen bagged grocery store varieties are a good choice, as freezing keeps produce just as fresh as it was on the farm the day of harvest.
- At the end of the day, it's all about, "calories in, calories out." If you count the calories while steering clear of too much fat, you'll remain healthy and avoid becoming overweight.
- Cardiovascular exercise will burn off any extra calories from fat.
- Performing weightlifting and calisthenics will enhance your strength and grow your muscles, but won't help you lose weight at all. That's what the treadmill is for.
- Shortening and margarine are healthier to use than most oils and butter because they're lower in saturated fat.
- Saturated fats and high cholesterol levels are what cause heart attacks.

- Eggs are high in cholesterol, therefore unhealthy. They should be eaten sparingly.
- High fructose corn syrup isn't harmful, and is nutritionally no different than table sugar.

I think we've heard enough.

One phrase that has become painfully and embarrassingly blasted within social media is:

"Because science!"

T shirts, memes, and even political disputes have flaunted this phrase for years as a supposedly infallible closing argument, but...

No.

science

noun
/ sī-ən(t)s /

1. study of the natural world based on facts learned through experiments and observation.

With such a vague primary definition, the *reputability* of scientific findings will depend largely on how experienced the involved scientists are, how skillfully the observations are made, and the extensiveness of the tests at hand.

Our government once hired those affiliated with a company that produces chemicals used for genetically modified plant seeds... to determine if said chemicals were safe for humans.

Well, of *course* they were proclaimed to be harmless.

"Because science!"

Shady? Questionable? Infuriating?

Biased?

Once the proclaimed science was challenged by independents *not* on the same payroll, the chemicals were absolutely found to be harmful, and lawsuits were thrown like darts.

"Science" is a word that's tossed around often in the world of law, politics, and social media debates, and in reality is quite meaningless when used in this exploitative manner.

George Washington was killed due to complications from a throat infection after having been treated with the oh-so-scientific medical practice of "bloodletting" — after which 40 percent of his blood had been drained out.

"Because science!"

Studies performed on products at clinics that have been funded purely *by* the pharmaceutical companies that have manufactured said drugs or products in question are often flaunted to support their efficacy.

"Because science!"

I am not suggesting that all scientific studies or findings are corrupt or without reputability, but one must consider the source.

By following the money trail, one can potentially sniff out, expose, and extinguish bias and corruption.

Some Better Science

The USDA's original food pyramid design was credited to Luise Light, a nutrition expert teaching at New York University in the early 1980's. Many sources indicate that her model had established that fresh whole vegetables, fruits, and lean meats should be the primary foods consumed.

Next up were modest amounts of dairy and whole grains, and finally nominal portions of processed carbohydrates and sugars.

The original pyramid would never be widely circulated to the public. Why?

It seems the food industries that were sitting on surpluses of processed corn and other cereal grains didn't like it very much.

What with the federal government not wanting to lose the huge dollars being funneled into the USDA by these companies, certain *modifications* to the pyramid were apparently made, and here we are today with over 40% of the citizens in our country suffering obesity.

Before the 1980s, it was less than 15%.

Purely circumstantial evidence? I wouldn't say so.

Dirty money influencing the government? I'd say so.

I've hired and spoken with many dietitians and nutritionists over the course of my life, resulting in me having read and learned more about nutrition than doctors do in medical school.

Don't be too impressed, it didn't take much.

Though curriculum is always evolving, most all of my primary care physicians over the years answered me personally that they'd spent a couple days at best learning about nutrition in medical school.

They'd primarily been taught the intricacies of bodily functions, and the affects of drugs on organ systems. Anatomy, Biochemistry, Microbiology, and Pharmacology are often touted.

The medical doctors I've lucked out with that *did* have substantial knowledge about nutrition mentioned having studied it independently, or in addition to their medical schooling.

This makes for a frustrating conversation when telling people what I'd learned after a latest visit to the nutritionist. They often come back with the same ignorant retort as they would when I'd return from a chiropractor:

"Why do you waste your money? You've been suckered! You *know* they're quacks, right? They haven't even been to medical school!"

They most certainly have *not* been to medical school to become chiropractors or nutritionists, because chiropractics and nutrition are not taught in medical school.

Medical school teaches largely of symptoms, drugs to prescribe for them, and when and how to do so.

This is not a smear against medical doctors or drugs.

We *need* medical doctors.

We *need* drugs.

When you're suffering an asthma attack, a medical doctor can quickly diagnose, provide, and prescribe effective drugs to help you breathe properly again.

You'll want that.

Do you think you have strep throat? A medical doctor can administer a test to find out, and *if so* can easily prescribe an effective antibiotic.

After taking drugs to address one's urgent, serious, or even life-threatening symptoms, it may be of great benefit to see a nutritionist to make any lifestyle changes that are causing or exacerbating these ailments.

I've been frustrated in the past by several medical doctors telling me directly that they don't recommend seeing a nutritionist or a chiropractor. They only suggest returning to them to address my general health if I feel anything is wrong.

I prefer not to operate in a purely retroactive manner, and I've been quick to change my PCP after having been given such biased advice.

I switched again a few years ago after I'd gone in for a very sore throat during allergy season. A throat culture was taken, and without waiting for the results, the doctor handed me two weeks worth of free samples of a common antibiotic.

"The test results won't be ready until after the weekend, but you can go ahead and start taking these now just in case it *really is* strep. If it's not, it won't cause any harm."

I didn't take it.

I sipped hot liquids all day to soothe my dry inflamed throat, and avoided unnecessary speaking until the following Tuesday when the results came through.

They indicated it was *not* strep, just a severely irritated throat from having sneezed a few hundred times in a day.

Ah, the joys of hay fever.

I'll now address that former list of atrocities with some information and knowledge I've obtained from none other than chiropractors, physical therapists, nutritionists, and finally — *respectable* medical doctors:

Addressing the Pant-load of Falsehoods

- There is rarely reason to take vitamins or supplements when these can be plentifully provided by proper foods, water, fresh air, sunlight, and exercise. Exceptions *can* apply when dealing with allergies, lifestyles of choice, rare conditions, or an intolerance.
- Large varieties of farm-fresh vegetables and fruits should be the most plentiful foods consumed. Though the vulnerability to, and impact of oxidation on different types of produce varies greatly, frozen vegetables are *far* from fresh, and often taste rancid or unpleasant.
- Processed grains have been substantially stripped of nutrients, thus having to be synthetically fortified with unnatural substances. Enjoying a fresh variety of whole grains will result in far greater nutritional benefits.
- Consuming calories from fat is *not* what causes one to gain weight.
- Selecting to eat foods labeled "low-fat" or "non-fat" have absolutely no direct or inherent correlation to whether or not one gains or loses weight.
- Protein is essential for a healthy, functional body. The amount required depends on the age, size, and activity level of each individual.
- Gaining weight is caused by consuming more calories than the body uses, thus getting stored as excess fat. The phrase "calories in, calories out" is accurate in this respect, but counting calories alone will not result in losing weight because not all calories are processed by the body equally. The human body is not a bomb calorimeter.

- Low to moderate intensity cardiovascular exercise combined with mild calisthenics will very efficiently burn fat, while medium to high intensity cardio will exercise the heart muscle. *Too much* intensity over time may cause damage.
- Performing weightlifting and calisthenics will both build muscle *and* burn fat, greatly improving your metabolism with a consistent routine.
- Maintaining the same moderate speed on a treadmill for long periods of time is a terribly inefficient workout.
- Shortening and margarine are arguably worse for the body due to hydrogenated oils and trans fats. Despite saturated fats, using modest amounts of healthier oil such as coconut or olive oil, and real grass-fed butter from your local farm will have far less risk of damaging the body than synthetic alternatives. They're also shown to provide clear benefits.
- Saturated fats alone (when used in moderation) do not cause heart attacks.
- High cholesterol alone does not cause heart attacks. Low-density lipoprotein (LDL cholesterol) will cause fatty build-up within arteries when affected by oxidation — primarily caused by excessive levels of simple sugars in the system and lack of proper nutrient intake.
- Eggs contain greater levels of high-density lipoprotein (HDL, not LDL) and are generally not considered a high cholesterol risk.
- High fructose corn syrup is a synthetic substance, and — much like processed white table sugar — is highly inflammatory and dangerously addictive. Both are a far cry from natural, unprocessed sugar. Perhaps the biggest threat of high fructose corn syrup is the fact that it's added to a large variety of processed foods to enhance flavors and extend their shelf life. It may be found in wheat crackers, whole grain cereals, luncheon meats, canned soups, condiments, hamburger buns, and more.

Whilst living in Oregon, I had developed a Vitamin D deficiency, which isn't uncommon in places where the sun shines sparsely. I ended up taking D3 supplements until I moved back to California.

Keeping a large variety of local veggies on our plate along with nuts, seeds, fresh local dairy products, and quality pastured lean meats has me consistently losing weight and feeling more energetic.

Learning to enjoy a wide variety of vegetables was a slow process for me, as lettuce, broccoli, and carrots were pretty much my only go-to's throughout childhood.

Once I started buying my own groceries, I experimented by branching out to some uncommon choices like okra, brussels sprouts or asparagus, but I'd sadly chosen to shop from the freezer section. This had established in me a strong distaste for many vegetables, associating them with rubber textures and chalky flavors.

Fresh veggies or bust.

We aren't sticklers about buying organic labels, either. When we shop at farmers' markets, we simply buy the cleanest, freshest produce we can find.

It wasn't until I was 31 years old when I had learned from a nutritionist that it was my constant effort to eat fat-free or low-fat foods that was thwarting my attempts to lose weight.

What I'd actually been doing was buying processed foods marketed as "low-fat", meanwhile being pumped full of sodium, processed carbohydrates, fillers, and chemical flavorings. All these elements were working together to keep me hungry and consuming a much higher number of calories than I would have if I'd been sated.

Along with the discovery of using CBD to address my chronic back pain, satiety turned out to be a huge factor of my weight loss success after it was explained how the body processes different foods.

The "calories in, calories out" phrase is often combated with, "a calorie is not a calorie" to demonstrate that the body handles 200 calories from a doughnut differently than those from from a handful of almonds.

I'm not a fan of either of these phrases.

The first, because: Not only are different types of foods not all handled the same way by the body, but it's very difficult to measure exactly how many calories the body burns off within a given time frame.

Consumer-level fitness devices and apps are anything but accurate.

The reason I disagree completely with the second phrase is: A calorie *is* indeed a calorie.

Always.

A calorie is a measurement. It's a word. It has a definition:

calorie

noun
/ kal'-ə-rē /

1. the amount of energy needed to raise the temperature of 1 kilogram of water through 1° Celsius.

A device called a "bomb calorimeter" had long been used to determine the calorie count of foods. A food would be burned as fuel using a controlled, electrical energy source, and when enough heat was generated by the fuel being burned to raise the temperature of 1000 grams of water by 1 degree Celsius, that amount of food burned was defined as 1 calorie.

The human stomach does not contain a laboratory-controlled consistently performing energy source, and one's metabolism is greatly affected by age, sex, muscle mass, activity level, body fat percentage, the actual foods consumed, and more.

It's no simple subject to explore.

What *is* simple is that foods that come in cans, cartons, bags, or boxes are typically highly processed and contain many ingredients that *slow* the metabolism, *deprive* the body of what it needs, and pump it full of things it *doesn't*.

Buying whole foods such as intact fruits and veggies, whole nuts and seeds, local farm-fresh dairy products, and pastured lean meats are about as favorable as nutrients can come.

One needs simply to learn to cook.

I suggest taking a local cooking class that teaches the basics, or heading to the library or bookstore to hunt down a book or two if on a tight budget.

With a little practice, healthy cooking can be a blast, and your body and mind will thank you.

iii

It's Okay, They're Natural Killers

I was in seventh grade when I first heard the term, "organic produce."

Two high school students had just walked into our social studies class at Solvang Elementary. They were members of the National Future Farmers of America Organization. They'd come to show us a documentary, and give a presentation about farming to the class.

The documentary ran about 20 minutes, and featured several short interviews with many employees on a small farm that flaunted organic produce.

Their business was genuine. They were a staff of few and went out of their way to showcase their organized array of crops, constantly dropping buzzwords while reminding the viewers often: "This is organic produce — we use *no* pesticides on our farm..."

After the presentation, FFA sign-up forms were left in the classroom for those interested, and every student was to write a paragraph about what they'd learned.

A few were chosen to read theirs out loud.

Every student's takeaway from that documentary was that organic farms were defined as *not* using genetically modified organisms (GMOs) and *not* using pesticides.

It wasn't until decades later that I learned the latter was untrue.

The documentary had been slyly edited and craftily scripted. The phrase, "This is organic produce — we use *no* pesticides on our farm..."

was no lie, but it just so happened to be that particular farm's practice; organic farms are absolutely permitted to use pesticides, and many do.

The use of *synthetic* pesticides is forbidden, as are hormones, and antibiotics in the raising of livestock and other aspects.

Naturally-occurring pesticides are absolutely allowed.

Many peoples' minds are blown when telling them pesticides are indeed used in organic farming. Some are too shocked to believe it, telling me that not wanting pesticides is the whole reason they buy organic, and they *know* that I must be mistaken.

I am not.

Others identify the word "natural" and incorrectly associate it with "harmless."

That's absurd — natural has *never* implied harmless.

Arsenic is natural. Cyanide is natural.

Granted, these are extreme examples, and not involved in organic farming, but my point has been made: The pesticides used are not inherently harmless.

After all, *"-cide"* is from Latin, *"to kill."*

Though the greatest risk of anyone experiencing adverse effects is actually to the farmers *themselves* (by inhaling large quantities of the stuff, or experiencing prolonged exposure to the skin), I'd still prefer my produce be grown using only proper amounts of soil, water, and sunlight.

Specific food-grade waxes are permitted in organic farming, and though they're non-toxic, they'll add a foul and bitter taste to your foods that you've now paid top dollar for because of a label.

Many who are already in the know of these above tidbits still rely on buying organic produce to ensure they are avoiding genetically engineered foods. However, the organic label is also used on many foods of which have no genetically engineered counterpart in the first place. This serves as a fabulous method of boosting sales while charging more for a product.

The price of organic certification has risen sharply, so much in fact that many previously certified farms have dropped the label — weary from being nickel-and-dimed by more costly and frequent inspections over the years.

Using creative marketing alternatives, many can been seen opting for a few more words on their signs:

"We grow our produce with soil, sun, and water."

"No GMOs used!"

"No pesticides of any kind!"

"No chemicals pumped into our soil!"

"No waxes!"

"We spray nothing but water on our plants!"

Their produce is fresh, high quality, absolutely delicious, and unlike organic standards has *no* pesticides or wax.

One doesn't have to "buy organic" to obtain high quality, healthy food.

That being said, some conventional produce is often the same price as organic in our local grocery store, and in such cases I'll usually opt for the latter of the two if prices are equal.

Nevertheless, I prefer buying straight from the farm, as the only likely way one will top that level of freshness is to grow it at home.

That's not happening in my apartment.

That is, aside from those peppers I plan to grow on the porch next spring...

I'm stoked.

iv

Stoners' Disappointment

It took me years to get over the stigma regarding marijuana that had been firmly instilled in me by the D.A.R.E. program back in elementary school.

"Cannabis destroys your life."

"Marijuana is a gateway drug."

"At first it's one joint. Next it's heroin and PCP."

After years of suffering debilitating chronic back pain resulting from a car accident, I finally gave a cannabis product a try once over-the-counter pain killers were no longer able to provide decent relief.

I'm talking about CBD. Cannabidiol.

Can-uh-bid-DYE-ull.

CBD does not cause intoxicating or psychoactive effects. That's produced by THC, which is mainly found in the flowers of marijuana plants. Some CBD oil is present in flowers, but is also found in the leaves and stems of the entire plant.

CBD doesn't get you high.

Many athletes have sworn by its painkilling and anti-inflammatory properties for years, while some scientific studies constantly conflict, resulting in CBD being unfairly branded as a placebo.

Wouldn't you know it, *those* studies attempting most desperately to debunk the efficacy of CBD products are often conducted and/or funded by those linked to pharmaceutical companies…

"Because Science!"

I can profess via personal experience that not only can CBD work, but it can work better than any over-the-counter drugs I've tried for my neck pain and lower back spasms.

I'm able to work, drive, and operate heavy machinery with unhindered focus.

I say it *can* work because I've tried no less than 30 different brands of CBD tinctures or edible products, all certified as "THC-Free." About 20 of these were completely useless as they did absolutely nothing to provide me with any pain relief.

As for the cause of this, serious studies are still quite lacking.

Perhaps a specific strain was ineffective?

Maybe the product was expired or old?

Could I have been swindled?

(Did some in reality contain no CBD at all?)

I kept track of each brand and product, the dose I took, if I'd taken it after having eaten a meal vs. on an empty stomach, and the results were consistent for each, respectively.

The brands that worked worked.

The brands that didn't didn't.

That's not even close to how the concept of a placebo works.

What I did find out is that my favorite brand — due to quality, value, and availability — is that from freestyle motocross professional Carey Hart: HartLuck CBD.

He *knows* a thing or two about pain management.

I don't smoke weed despite the many available high-CBD strains nearly devoid of THC. Lit marijuana smells to me like a mixture of angry skunk, dank locker room, and a dumpster fire.

No sir, I don't like it.

Thankfully, HartLuck CBD tincture has been the stench-free catalyst that has allowed me to function normally without pain.

I've been able to increase my mobility and establish an exercise program decades after suffering my aforementioned car accident.

Of course, sitting in a chair for my day job for over 20 years didn't help things.

It turns out that's unhealthy.

Even medical doctors and specialists alike have dropped the phrase to me, "sitting is the new smoking," due to the increase in ailments they're professing to see from prolonged sitting habits of the latest generations.

I truly hope the taboo surrounding CBD and medical marijuana continues to decrease in the future, because nominal *and* crooked scientific efforts are disgracefully depriving those in need of an effective treatment.

V

My Diet Is Trendier Than Your Diet

Have you ever sunk your teeth into a yellow colored treat, be it hard candy, taffy, or ice cream, expecting to taste lemon only to find it's in fact banana flavored?

I like lemons. I like bananas, too. Yet, an expectation of one flavor whilst being delivered another can be rather surprising or deceiving.

To me, that's what has always been the main deterrent of food alternatives.

This isn't a smear on gluten-free, grain-free, dairy-free, vegetarian, vegan, or any other diets at all.

It absolutely is, mind you, a call-out and quick little commentary on their *marketing:*

It's appalling.

I rather enjoy cornbread, cauliflower, fermented soybean products, cashews, nutritional yeast, and basil.

That being said, if you bake those ingredients into a round shape and tell me to try a bite of your Margherita Pizza, I'm probably going to wince, gag, gulp it down uncomfortably, and then ask you what on earth it *really* is...

Because that's absolutely not a Margherita Pizza.

Please: Stop marketing things to be what they don't even slightly resemble, mkay?

I can't tell you how many times I grin and shake my head after a proclaimed life-long vegan swears that their miracle brand hamburger tastes just like the real thing.

Tell me — how on earth would a life-long vegan possibly know that?

Expectation set, expectation not met.

I highly suspect the sales of these trendy diets' many falsely advertised foods are often so successful because they're banking on some very common human emotions and behaviors.

They're exploiting weaknesses, if you will.

In particular: pretentiousness, insecurity, addiction, lack of willpower, and low self-esteem.

It's dastardly.

*"If you buy our product, you can eat **more** of it! After all, if it's organic / low-carb / keto / vegan / vegetarian / grain-free / gluten-free, then that means it's healthy!"*

I've fluctuated from being slightly overweight to obese and back again since the late fifth grade, as I'd found eating sugars, processed carbohydrates, and overly salted snacks made me feel incredible.

As the elementary school outcast, I could sit in front of the TV at home watching my favorite shows or playing video games with nobody in the room shouting insults my way while I emptied bags and bowls of snacks repeatedly.

It's a fantastic way of getting a dopamine high.

It's also a fantastic way of gaining weight.

This is where the dark truth of trendy diets comes into play, and it's most despicable.

If we're being honest with ourselves, we all know what foods are nutritious and which aren't. We're aware that balanced meals prepared at home from whole, farm-fresh ingredients are the way to go, but *that* takes time, practice, and skill.

Excessive sugar, salt, and fried foods are unhealthy, but it's much *easier* to grab a box or a bag and have a quick meal ready in minutes, right?

I think it sure is.

It's even better when said box has a newly hyped trendy little label or tagline that indicates adherence to the rules of a marketed diet!

This grants us the joyful advantage of boasting to friends and family that we're now better than they are, along with the bonus of lying to ourselves.

"If it's on a point system, it's healthy..."

On many such "systems," one can suffer eating bland salads all day long so they can scarf a half pint of ice cream and a doughnut at night to still come in under the daily point limit.

I know a lot of people that have been on point systems for decades, and they're still suffering.

"If it's gluten-free, it's healthy..."

There are plenty of gluten-free snacks, fried foods, and bags of salty carbs just waiting to be devoured at every grocery store in the country.

"Low-carb is the best diet..."

Several people at a former place of employment went through a phase in which they microwaved bacon strips all day, and ate a paltry salad at dinnertime alongside more bacon. It's low-carb, so that meant they were eating healthy, right?

Not all, but *several* of them ended up malnourished and ill after a couple months. One was even hospitalized with mild damage to several organs from their poor decisions.

"Vegan/Grain-Free/Keto diets have far superior health benefits..."

Anywhere you wish to look, you can find vegan, grain-free and keto varieties of beer, doughnuts, ice cream, pizza, cookies, cereals, soft pretzels, crackers, chips, and processed snacks galore.

There's nothing universally "superior" about the keto diet. It's merely one method of eating that tricks the body into strongly prioritizing the burning of fat instead of carbohydrates. As with any low-carb diet, keeping the body in an extended state of ketosis while failing to observe proper nutrition has the ability to cause some serious damage to the body — *far beyond* the liver.

There's nothing "beneficial" about abstaining from quality whole grains unless you have an intolerance. It's otherwise nullifying a bountiful source of fiber and nutrients.

There's nothing "healthy" by definition about veganism; it means abstaining from animal products, and nothing more.

Granted, there's no denying it: Eating poor quality, unethically raised, highly processed animal products can *absolutely* cause harm to the body — not inherently because they're animal products, but because they're highly processed, inflammatory, contain excessive additives, and lacking in nutrients.

There's a decent chance they're being consumed in excess, as well.

Italy, Spain, and Greece have held long histories as countries with an average life expectancy of over 80 years, and none of their societies within are universally vegan, gluten-free, grain-free, *or* low-carb.

It seems there *is* one important element these countries do have in common: Their cultures are rich with a history of eating whole, fresh foods from local farms and waters.

Modern scientists coined the trendy phrase "Mediterranean Diet" to slap a label on the eating style of these countries, but it's no fleeting trend. It's no diet. *They* just call it food.

Looking at the habits of France, another country well-known for long life, one can quickly see that universally fearing saturated fat is another mistake.

Granted, the French too greatly respect and embrace local produce, eating an *exponentially* higher percentage of fresh vegetables, fruits, and fermented dairy products than Americans. They also eat smaller portions of (while not abstaining from) meat and fish.

Struggling as I've been with that addiction to processed carbs established in my early childhood, I can tell you firsthand that nothing about any of the aforementioned trends is inherently healthy.

They don't work by principle.

People still often believe what they wish, and on a very rare occasion we might meet somebody who professes, "I embraced this trend diet and lost 100 pounds, gained muscle, and I'm now in the best shape of my life!"

In truth, they didn't improve their health because of embracing a trend diet; they actually learned about nutrition, started eating healthy foods, nixed the junk, and engaged in proper exercise.

These are completely different concepts.

These diets have done little more than enabled people suffering addiction to unhealthy foods to keep eating them in large quantities, and to do so with a newfound sense of justification.

Looking at myself in the mirror for decades, I can assure you that none of them work, and sooner or later one needs to address the addiction.

It's slow, difficult, painful, takes discipline, is unpleasant, brings about irritability and frustration, and may possibly serve as one of the most difficult things for you to accomplish in life.

Any box on a shelf that proclaims otherwise is looking to take your money.

vi

Keeping Your Wits

Mental health is another subject with a nasty stigma.

Psychologists (behavioral and talk therapists) and Psychiatrists (the former combined with medical diagnoses and drug therapy) have both become associated only with the most severe mental afflictions portrayed to the extreme by The Media.

Many conditions are often mocked.

These jests have given way to many sufferers becoming too reluctant to seek much-needed help.

A mark of shame or that of an outcast even appears to have been issued frequently among former generations, and if anything, *shame on them* for letting ego supersede positive support for loved ones in need.

I was assigned to the resident elementary school campus psychologist for two sessions per week, shortly after moving to Solvang. My inability to cope with constant bombardment of insults and verbal bullying from the student body had left me silent, depressed, and unmotivated to do homework.

My grades had started to suffer.

That wasn't me. I had formally been a straight-A student throughout nearly my entire elementary school tenure.

The psychologist was very helpful, giving me a primer on the very basics of human behavior and letting me in on the real reasons that younger masses usually lash out:

Insecurity, jealousy, lack of attention, poor self-esteem, tough family life, *no family life*...

As was predicted by the psychologist, the more I found out about the worst offenders, they'd been revealed to have had terrible parents or suffered adversities of their own that had not yet been dealt with. In turn, this prompted them to either become aggressive or behave in a recklessly self-destructive manner.

Some of them went on to have criminal records, and that's a shame, but most all of them wised up after getting the help they needed.

One doesn't need to resemble a cartoon character wearing a straight jacket in a padded room to benefit from mental health experts.

People deserve to be at peace, and there are many professionals available who are trained to help them get there.

Sometimes, a little moral support goes a long way.

Next Moves

Eating to acquire nutrients, and exercising to maintain physical well-being are acts that support both quality of life, and the overall health of one's entire body and mind.

Finding pleasure in cooking and physical activities served as a key element for me in heading toward the right direction.

Facing the fact that there are no shortcuts was another.

I'm concerned for future generations of America, as it seems there's no slowing the large scale farming industries that continue to pump out the lowest quality produce the planet has ever seen, while daring to call it "food."

These unnatural substances are hardly fit to be consumed by any living creature, and it doesn't exactly do the planet very well, either.

The nightly news and social media headlines have for years been touting fearsome seasonal viruses and violent crimes as the primary attention-getters.

Meanwhile, the exponentially more dangerous top causes of death that are largely *nutritionally* related (Heart Disease, Stroke, COPD, Type 2 Diabetes, and several types of Cancer), conveniently go without mention.

What does get mentioned is a several minute long commercial for the next miracle drug to keep bodies functioning while allowing people to maintain sedentary lifestyles and poor eating habits.

Perhaps this very young and belovéd country of America might look toward those like Spain, Italy, Greece, France, and Iceland, who have long established superior nutritional habits, farming methods, and respectful environmental practices that could be greatly learned from by all.

In the meantime, I'm continuing my personal interests and self-education in cooking, supporting local farms, and occasionally checking in with a physical therapist to make sure I'm exercising properly to not hurt myself.

I only wish I'd started sooner.

6
That Digital Abyss

A Gift and a Curse

In my youth, I'd have memorized at any given time no less than 20 phone numbers of family, friends, and local businesses that I frequented.

Now I only memorize Kelly's and my own. All the others are stored on my mobile device, and backed up to my email account.

Many of my favorite restaurants and businesses from my childhood have closed.

Several friends have changed carriers and phone numbers multiple times throughout the last couple of decades, so The Internet has proven a rather convenient method of staying in touch.

Shopping online has also been a great advantage, especially while living in a small town. It's nearly 40 miles from our apartment to the closest shopping mall, so it's nice to purchase appliances, electronics, media, and clothing with a couple of clicks to have it arrive days later.

It's a *huge* saver of transportation costs.

Online videos continue to prove incredible opportunities for learning, many of which are free of charge.

Remarkable as it can be at times, this digital realm is not without its shortcomings.

An offer for a job interview in the summer of 2020 was nearly botched for me. Despite using one of the most popular and reliable free email providers available, a message from a prospective employer experienced nearly a three day delay before being delivered to my Inbox.

I had been checking this email account daily in a desktop browser, as well as had the email app actively running in the background on my mobile device twenty-four seven.

I take job applications quite seriously.

I accepted the interview a mere few hours away from the deadline, apologizing for the late response and explaining I'd only just received the email that afternoon.

Though attending multiple remote interviews that went very comfortably, that company ended up selecting another applicant for the position. I highly suspect my less than prompt response to that initial email had perhaps contributed to my being passed up.

Irritated, I *did* perform basic online troubleshooting by reporting the issue to the email provider and scouring their community forums as to try preventing future occurrences of the behavior.

I quickly found out that I wasn't alone. Many had been reporting random message delays without discovered causes or resolutions for quite some time — over 11 months.

All the provider had yet done was announce that they were working on a fix, and estimated less than 0.5% of their customer base had experienced these sporadic delays.

Lucky me.

Technical issues and software hiccups will always exist, but they don't often faze me. I usually proclaim to owe that to the fact that I was born in 1980.

Generation X was *nearly* the last batch of young adults to really experience what life in America was like before the digital realm completely enveloped entertainment, communication, and the business world.

The first phone I used was a landline rotary phone.

My first television was an old black and white 13" hand-me-down with no remote control, and no coaxial input. I had to use a screwdriver to attach a 300-to-75 ohm matching transformer so I could connect my Nintendo Entertainment System.

That's right, I would play The Legend of Zelda, Super Mario Brothers, Metroid, and Kid Icarus in black and white.

I mastered the art of using the TV's single antenna for signal reception. Bunny ears would have been an upgrade.

It functioned well enough; I got a couple channels that allowed me to catch my favorite shows after school, and Looney Tunes and some sitcoms after dinner.

I used 5 ¼" floppy discs for computer software, and cartridges for video games.

Albums were played on vinyl and cassette, and some family and friends still had 8-track decks in their cars.

My family purchased our first VCR in 1987 alongside the first home release of Disney's *Lady and the Tramp* on VHS.

I regularly looked up phone numbers and addresses in the phone book.

I used encyclopedias for knowledge reference, and flipped through atlases and road maps to familiarize myself with my hometown.

I never had a question of where I was going, with who, or at what time before I left the house.

Today, most everything remains the same for me.

It's only when I'm involving several other people in my activities that I'm left wondering often until the last minute where on earth they've decided to eat, and what the transportation plans are.

Yes, it's mildly annoying, but they're family and friends. I know how to exercise patience.

(Rotary phones, TV antennas, and manual VCR tracking, remember?)

I often leave my cell phone on silent. I've even left it at home on occasion only to have some surrounding friends or family emit a shocked gasp as they proclaim in a fluster, "You didn't bring your phone! What are you going to *do* all day?!"

Perhaps relax and enjoy life? Live independently and with confident self-reliance like I did in the '80s and '90s?

The *sheer panic* that comes over peoples' faces when they realize they've left their cell phone at home, or even in the car when at a grocery store or restaurant, astounds me.

It's as if they've had their life force cut off.

They don't know how to behave or function.

Cold sweats, anxiety, and insecurity take over as people scramble to remember where they've left their mobile device.

This behavioral development didn't happen overnight.

Society has been slowly distancing itself from proactive responsibility and self-reliance as new technology offered more opportunities to do so.

It's not the fault of technology *or* its inventors; it's been a free choice of every consumer to behave how they wish, always.

Shortly after moving to San Diego in late 2003, I'd learned that a certain favorite rustic-themed restaurant from my childhood had a location there in the county. I was excited to make a night of it when my friend Jay visited one weekend.

I looked up the restaurant in the phone book and dialed the number on my landline so that I wouldn't burn up my daytime cell phone minutes.

When an employee answered the phone and asked how they could help me, I requested a reservation for four people. As customary, the employee confirmed by repeating the date and time back to me along with my name and phone number I'd provided.

I then asked for directions for which exit to take, as I'd be driving westbound on the nearby highway.

They were completely stifled.

I ended up being put on hold twice for several minutes as this poor baffled human asked multiple coworkers how to get to the restaurant from the only nearby highway — the same restaurant they themselves were standing in and working at.

Another employee finally came to the phone and assured me they'd worked there for *years,* and could absolutely help me with the directions to their establishment.

They told me which exit to take, gave the names of two streets to turn on, and let me know that I'd then see their building on the right side.

They ended the call by apologizing that I'd waited so long to be provided directions, suggesting next time it may be easier to look it up on The Internet.

Their inflection was slightly condescending, as to *really* say, "Why did you bother calling us instead of looking online?"

Gee, I guess I didn't realize how *silly* it was of me to think that calling a human who was actually working on site at the restaurant in question would be faster and more reliable, but I digress...

Not feeling an excess of confidence in the employee after hanging up the phone, I sighed as I turned on my computer, dialed up my internet connection, launched Netscape, then navigated to the MapQuest website to verify the directions.

After taking about 10 minutes to perform the above, I had them.

It turned out that the name of the exit I'd been given *didn't exist* driving westbound on the highway, and this local employee that had proclaimed to have worked there for years got the name of the restaurant's cross street wrong by several blocks.

Later that night (after following the accurate directions that I'd obtained myself), Jay and I arrived right on time for our reservation only to be told by the hostess that it didn't exist.

They had no reservation on record at all with my name or phone number. Ah, but they *were* generous enough to put us on the waiting list...

It was currently a 90 minute wait, as Friday night means party time in San Diego county.

We ended up going to a nearby In-N-Out Burger instead, and were thoroughly enjoying delicious classic burgers and fries 15 minutes later.

I love In-N-Out.

Now, keep in mind that this particular pathetic failure in very basic customer service happened in 2003, and it consisted of an employee proclaiming to be proficient, but ended up suggesting I verify the provided information by using The Internet.

I'd been calling places on the phone to ask for directions throughout the '90s, and people were for the most part always right on top of things.

They'd provide a confident answer complete with accurate street names, and sometimes even descriptions of landmarks for easy points of reference.

That had already drastically changed by 2003, and that reservation debacle was far from the first time something like that had occurred.

It had been slowly happening for a couple years, and was getting worse.

Whenever I hear people blaming the recent pandemic for poor customer service experiences and lower quality products and services today, I wince.

It's been happening *long* before these events; lockdown has little to do with it, but it serves as a convenient scapegoat.

Many people have slowly but surely allowed themselves to become excessively dependent on The Internet just to *function* in their daily lives, and they're noticeably slipping on the punctuality front.

I had a total of five remote webcam interviews for two different positions at the same company last year, and I was logged in and connected to every single session with my headset mic and camera active no less than five whole minutes early.

I'd sip my mug of water, sitting and smiling patiently on the air.

The hosts were no less than four minutes late for every single interview, and once kept me waiting for nearly 10 minutes past the scheduled time.

I'd expected better.

As harmful as laziness is to quality progress, it isn't the only ugly trait that's made an increased appearance over the years.

A far worse craze has grown over recent decades that was once rightly frowned upon.

Aside from the many that have become all too reliant on The Internet for basic tasks, others are obsessed with making absolutely certain to have their egos stroked on an hourly basis.

Deeming it far more important to maintain the impression of appearing superior rather than actually being correct, this behavior prevents everyone involved from achieving productivity in any fashion.

It's a craze that's lead society into a ditch of late, but with a little tact and a touch of intelligence, together we can calmly extinguish these acts of digital arson...

Mob Mentality and Cowardice at Their Finest

"Keyboard warriors."
"Hashtags."
"Triggered."
"Doomscrolling."
"Snowflakes."
"Privileged."
"Cancel culture."
"Woke..."

So very many hyped buzzwords oozing with the pus of excessive indignation have infested The Internet in recent years, accomplishing little more than deepening the grooves of infantile rifts within society.

In the world of modern social media, many justice warriors are self-proclaimed — much like that of a presumptuous intermediate musician introducing themselves as a virtuoso.

Shooting poisonous barbs of sardonic aggression back and forth from the *furthest* opposing standpoints, these extremist attack dogs participate in frequent urination contests with the primary goal of being crowned champions of their cult for the day.

All the while, they consistently fail to catch on that their actions resemble those of an inept band of stranded, bickering children struggling to govern themselves on a remote island.

Double standards and hypocrisy commonly make up the foundation of social media arguments, and a lumpy drywall paste of spite serves to coat their structural frames built of ignorance.

Easily "triggered" when confronted with facts and objectivity, these martyrs are quick to methodically utilize their trade tools of redirection, *misdirection,* and blame games as to distract from their lack of expertise on every topic of consequence.

This suffices to avoid even *their own* realization that they themselves either have nothing worth listening to, and/or possess no actual experience or ability to resolve any situation at hand...

Quite like televised political debates.

It's all a fine treat, but it doesn't stop there.

If for some reason anybody finds a few brief seconds to drop even nominal facts or snippets of respectable science to these types, they'll be quick to delete those comments and block that person from their page.

-----
*It's much easier to hide from
reality and reason than to confront them.*

This fortitude-lacking act of ghosting or blocking other users *does* take a toll on the conscience of the outwardly divine, so some damage control must be done to again raise their own spirits after such an ordeal.

When some time has passed without being engaged with a "like" or "repost" of their scattered vitriol, witch-hunts will then be organized and carried out by said warriors in order to stir another pot.

Whether using a hackneyed political meme or a biased slight against another party's agenda serving as bait for arguments, the show must go on in order to fuel their own gaping self-esteem shortage.

"Doomscrolling," the act of obsessively dwelling on and seeking out pessimistic news articles and social media posts one after another, also contributes nothing but woe.

To many, this negative behavior is regrettably infectious and will frequently set off their cult's *other* followers to either share said post, or embrace their personal anger and contempt to fabricate one of their own.

They'll attack and publicly berate people for brands and materials of clothing they wear, apps they use, retailers they support, cars they drive, foods they eat, and other social media pages they follow.

They'll even act as pet and parent police by judging others' family photos and video clips out of context.

Opinions of others will not be respected, but quickly put down and perhaps be used as grounds for another dismissal from their friends list.

It was years ago that I first voiced my disapproval of the freshly passed Affordable Care Act. On my own social media page, I had professed the act to be poorly implemented because it caused many people substantially life-changing hardships.

Though it had helped millions of *some* Americans by making select improvements to an already broken system, it literally took away millions of *other* Americans' already insufficient health care plans, and the ability to afford one going forward.

This is fact. It's objective.

Whether people choose to acknowledge it or not — it actually happened, and millions of hard working Americans including myself still suffer daily in chronic pain because of it.

One of my coworkers and a good friend of several years at the time had seen that post. Without any warning signs, attempts to learn more details about my perspective, or even to express concern for a friend who was now clearly living in significantly intense physical pain, he added the first comment to my post:

"DE-FRIEND INCOMING!"

He indeed removed me from his friends list within the hour, and since that day has never spoken to me again.

That's all it took.

It was as if he *assumed* I'd wished ill will on those that benefited from the act.

I never had.

My phone and text inquiries as to what it was that caused him to cut ties with me so abruptly went unanswered.

It was later learned from other coworkers that he spoke poorly of those who strayed from alignment in regards to any of his party views, and he'd been heard referring to *me* as a "far right wingnut" and "an extremist."

Was this because I wasn't *happy* with my medical insurance having been taken away and priced literally higher than my rent?

Others who had benefited from the act even went as far to accuse me of being "narcissistic" and thinking only of myself.

In psychology, that's known as projecting.

I didn't understand where any of this was coming from, but it absolutely revealed how they themselves regarded the suffering of others.

A number of years after that unfriendly fallout, a certain Republican elect had adopted the regular practice of taking to social media to spout off in a belligerent, childish manner. It continued frequently to the point of their being banned from the privately owned platform.

This is fact. It's objective.

Whether people choose to acknowledge it or not — it actually happened, and The People suffered further polarization while the perceived impression of the average American by other countries went further into the toilet because of it.

Ask around.

When I'd posted that this politician's behavior and the whole ordeal itself was an embarrassment, I was suddenly accused of being a "crazy anti-conservative liberal" who was apparently "against freedom of speech."

It was as if they *assumed* I was glad he'd been censored, and that I was against people being able to speak their mind.

I am not.

These were more ignorant assumptions; I'm strongly against censorship. After all...

-----

*The identity of a fool is most
easily revealed by their own tongue.*

I'm registered as non-partisan.

In a variety of elections, I've voted for some Democrats, some Republicans, Independents, Libertarians, Socialists, and even those from the Green party.

I vote by the *individual* — not by the letter of the confounded party next to their name.

Why had I been filed away as a "far right wingnut" by one, and a "crazy anti-conservative liberal" by another?

One can't truly be both, but one can certainly be *neither*.

This accusatory behavior isn't unheard of. In fact, it's rather common.

If those who've become extreme party loyalists wish to remain within their cultist circles of praise, they must remain concretely devout.

Any who stray from, disagree with, or disapprove of *any element* of their party representatives' agendas shall be socially targeted and verbally attacked with the full fervor of the cult, and quickly labeled "one of them..."

A member of the opposing primary party.

The enemy.

They shall abide no instances of individual thought. Any possible reality of other voters expressing open-minded thinking without allowing a political party to dictate their every move may possibly shatter these loyalists' fragile world of insecurity.

You *must* be labeled one or the other.

This act of baiting and berating others on a gut-reaction has seemingly become an online sport over the years, fueling egos and inciting fiery feuds that only result in reinforcing oppositions.

Social media — heck, *all* of The Media has been a hot zone for far too long.

Lack of both patience and clarity within communications doesn't help.

Hashtags are a painful example of this.

I'm not saying they can't serve a positive purpose. They increase visibility of posts and blogs, and can circulate healthy topics and ideas.

They can also spread fear, incite mob mentality, cause confusion, and separate The People with excessively vague taglines.

It's admittedly no different than any other aspect of media in this regard, but surely a new tool to be exploited.

Hashtags have even grown to represent status symbols.

People will frequently add hashtags for several different political, social, or lifestyle preferences to a posted photo of a sunset or bowl of ramen in order to garner more "likes" — as well as to condemn those who don't act likewise.

Enter "cancel culture."

Although the acts of ostracizing and boycotting aren't anything new by a long shot, The Internet has proven to be a tool that can be used by those most unsound and immature individuals as a powerful smear machine.

With the ability to hide behind the anonymity of a handle or avatar, people can now exercise their sanctimonious dominance over others by preaching with yellow journalism to a broad scope of strangers, all the way down to a personal level if they so please.

From outside the bias-sphere, this has a great resemblance to a rumor mill in elementary school:

Toxic, fruitless, and destructive.

When one's goal is feeding the flames of fury brought on by ill levels of unchecked indignation, there remains no chance for resolve. There is room only for unbridled malice.

Learning to stop and look at not only the bigger picture, but the *self* is one lesson that might help extinguish the billowing flames of these social media warriors' egos, as opposed to them lashing out irrationally.

A very recent event comes to mind that had revealed much regarding the maturity level of these practitioners of spiteful scrutiny.

In mid 2021, the California DFEH (Department of Fair Employment and Housing) filed suit against Activision Blizzard, Inc. after a two-year investigation had reported allegedly blatant instances of discrimination and harassment against female employees.

That behavior by any company or individual is absolutely inexcusable, and was unfortunate to learn of.

I've been a fan of Blizzard's software titles for decades, as was mentioned in my first book, "True Tales from the Land of Digital Sand." I wrote how they'd provided great entertainment, and how *World Of Warcraft* in particular served as a great slice of adventure that helped me through some tough times.

I've spoken with several males and females over the years that have previously worked for Blizzard, specifically on the *WoW* team since 2004. Though they'd never mentioned any universal mistreatment in the past, that's beside the point.

It's being mentioned now, and it needs to be addressed.

As for by what manner or means — well, that seems to have opened up a digital can of worms all over The Internet.

One has to be careful who they're chatting with these days, as some people are getting pummeled and scolded within gaming chat rooms once it's revealed they're still playing any games developed by Blizzard Entertainment.

Clear and suitable action by the company to address the despicable mistreatment at hand has already been given sharp priority.

They're being sued.

Here, I'm addressing the hypocritical holier-than-thou act of negatively judging other people based on the services and products they've chosen to use.

Two of many glaring problems with this whole practice are:

1. Excessive self-righteousness → Martyrdom → Hasty judgment of others → Ironic self-incrimination.
2. Lack of personal consideration, and/or inability to step outside the bias-sphere.

The act of viewing the bigger picture has the tendency to incite positive reflection and self-improvement, inspiring respectful tolerance rather than biased reprehension.

I'll elaborate, being sure to use excessive amounts of dramatically gaudy formatting to try matching the benchmark fervor of the haughtily obstinate social media zealots.

This ought to be rich:

WoW: The Bigger Picture

Several of my friends and guild members who use Discord (messaging software) have recently been spotted asking other gamers if they're down to play some *World Of Warcraft* for an evening.

The others may then reply that they're *not subscribing* at the moment, because they're personally uncomfortable supporting Blizzard until the company announces "further action" to address the matter of sexual discrimination and harassment that's been brought to light.

What *level* of action this is... remains different for every individual's comfort zone.

The response is acknowledged by the inquiring gamer, and the day goes on without either party judging the other of being pretentiously superior, arrogant, ignorant, malodorous, or evil.

I feel exchanges like these described above are politely phrased, honorable, fair, and deserve to be respected.

Now, then — there are many points at which things have the tendency to go quickly down the porta-potty for both parties (say **that** 10 times fast!), but I've witnessed one scenario most frequently:

It's when excessive zeal, indignation, and disparagement are implemented to unfairly denounce and ostracize an **entire** company, its body of work, *and* its community.

I've seen a World of Warcraft guild's Discord server stained by those condemning them in numbers for playing *WoW* at this time, quick to be called *sexists* and *male chauvinists*.

This was a rather ignorant accusation, as the great majority of those active players... *happened to be female*.

Once they'd spoken up of their genders, this only exacerbated the situation with them being disparaged *further* by the prosecutors, in so many words being labeled as "turncoats" and "terrible people" on the grounds of personally enabling **unethical conduct of companies** for their own selfish convenience and recreation.

It seemed these pious accusers who had freely chosen not to support something had held the act of demanding others to *join them* — more important than their personal choice to not support something.

...They felt it necessary to conduct a witch-hunt.

No good came of it, members were kicked out of the Discord server in droves, and a *new* server was created by invitation only — by the female guild captain.

Here's where I see painful irony having come into play:

To bring such judgment upon others in the manner of the above example is objectively hypocritical.

This is not merely because of that most nauseatingly humbling and trite reminder that we're all "only human," but rather *embarrassingly* because these acts of chastising are taking place by communicating with a piece of technological hardware that was in one manner or another, manufactured by way of **unethical conduct of companies.**

Many a technology company has been repeatedly exposed for use of child labor, and/or such poor working conditions resembling indentured servitude that they invoke acts of suicide in adults.

As mentioned a few chapters ago (and by the legendary Ricky Gervais during the 77th Golden Globe Awards...), far too many companies' manufacturing processes involve unspeakably deplorable treatment of employees and the environment alike in either material sourcing, processing, or assembly.

I've still not happened upon a 100% ethically produced computer or mobile device these days...

Shouldn't that make us *all* guilty of enabling **unethical conduct of companies** by the purchasing of these items for our own selfish convenience and recreation?

Does knowing that slavery and abuse are involved in their manufacturing yet *continuing to use them* make people any more or less terrible than continuing to play *WoW* upon hearing of the lawsuit at hand?

Are we to cease using ALL unethical products and services instantly upon discovery?

Instantly!?

If so, good luck getting to work, covering your naked body, communicating with many humans efficiently, making a dollar, or eating any food by **next month.**

I suppose if anything, by dictionary definition, these boycotts make one ignorant or — pretentious...

-----

*It's so **easy** to label oneself holier-than-thou, as long as one is boycotting things that aren't **inconvenient** to do so, **isn't** it?*

Should we all simply stop patronizing superstores that sell a single piece of clothing produced by Uyghur slaves from within the labor camps in Xinjiang or by children in sweat shops?

Are we to then conduct a witch-hunt to sniff out all **others** that still shop there?

Furthermore, do we barge in and interview every independent small business owner, grilling them about **every** facet of their conduct?

At what point does it stop?...

This is NOT to justify the mistreatment of humans, or the turning of a blind eye to inappropriate acts.

I myself have been the victim of sexual harassment countless times throughout my life by female *and* male coworkers, and action was taken every time by **promptly** reporting them to authorities.

This is NOT to justify a toxic, knee-jerk cancel culture.

I've witnessed acts beyond sexual harassment in the workplace involving violence, slander, theft... and have reported each instantly.

I made sure I did **everything** within my legal ability to weed out the trash, and do what should be done while remaining in my company's employ.

I don't believe that makes me a terrible person.

We may not have started the fires, but we can work together to extinguish them in a healthy manner.

This is about both short-term effective action to cease immediate harms, and a long-term strategy *(that actually gets carried out, not just planned for show...)* to exponentially improve conditions, services, and products as quickly and realistically as possible.

This is about looking at the bigger picture.

I wouldn't want to lose my job because of a boycott of my company versus taking out the trash.

I now know of only one female personally who works at Blizzard, and she hasn't had the universally jeered "frat boy" experience in her department. She wishes people wouldn't completely slam the *entire company* so. There are many great people she works with — male and female — on her own team and others.

I also personally know of only one male who works at Blizzard — or rather, *worked* at Blizzard. He'd suffered so much wrongful and unjust harassment from peers for remaining in their employ that he felt pressured enough to find another job.

He now works for Apple. How's ***that*** for irony?

I've even seen some comments on this matter — from adults — that go as far to proclaim they wouldn't resubscribe to *WoW* again until every male employee at Blizzard Entertainment was let go.

Per an article on The Internet from July 2021, Roughly 9,500 people are employed by Activision Blizzard, Inc, and about half of them work for Blizzard Entertainment in Irvine. That's a lot of humans.

Is it fair to assume that every male who works at Blizzard Entertainment has behaved inappropriately and deserves to be sacked?

If one chooses to embrace such an outlook, then... **Reality Check:** That's not just assumption; *that too* is sexual discrimination.

For nearly three decades, I've seen an incredible number of humans communicating on The Internet with ignorance and disrespect, and it gets worse every year.

I see people speaking to one another on social media, in chat rooms, in games, or during live feeds with conduct they'd ***never*** have the gall to exercise if the person they were addressing were standing in front of them.

This defines cowardice.

As stated, I try to make a point to communicate with text just the same as I would with my voice if the reader were present.

That's another flesh and blood human I'm communicating with, and one can ***certainly*** be respectful with little effort.

Let us hope these pathetic displays of infantile trivialities will soon have run their course, lest our wee toddler of a country be crushed by the weight of its own internal conflict and stubbornness.

The world is bigger than me.
May it be so for us all.

Not of Our Own Devices

Addiction doesn't discriminate. It affects all ages, genders, cultures, orientations, and waist sizes.

In restaurants, theaters, lobbies, city streets, country roads, passenger seats, and subway platforms, people everywhere can be seen with eyes glued to their phones.

A few weeks ago, Kelly and I enjoyed dinner for two at a local restaurant, and in the same dining room sat a middle aged party of six at a long adjacent table — every one of them with phones out, silent and staring.

All six of them.

Look, I realize not everybody feels like being social every moment of their lives.

I get it. I'm an introvert.

Being introverted doesn't mean one dislikes other people, has a short fuse, is eccentric or particular, socially awkward, or resemblant of any other negative stereotypes that have been ignorantly associated with the term.

To be an introvert means that sustained social interactions may possibly cause exhaustion over long periods; being around a large number of people all day will drain an introvert's energy, but spending some time relaxing alone with one's creative thoughts will recharge their batteries.

An extrovert will typically behave in an opposite fashion; they may quickly hit their limit of alone time before becoming restless, and will need to socialize in order to replenish their mental and emotional vitality.

Regardless of one's personality style, it strikes me as illogical and strange for several humans to be paying to gather for a meal at a large table in a public place designed to *fit* said capacity, all the while completely ignoring each others' presence.

Psst. Stay home and eat for 90% less, next time, folks!

Inside movie theaters, people can now be seen using their brightly lit mobile devices all the way up until the final preview trailer's end... maintaining the impression that such an act isn't rude or distracting if the main feature hasn't started yet.

I strongly disagree with their assessment.

It's rare even to complete a movie viewing at home among friends or family without somebody whipping out their smartphone to see what other films a familiar actor was in, or address a latest notification from one of many apps.

We've grown used to it. It's as if they can't help it. They *must know now!*

Even in my very small hometown of the Santa Ynez Valley, I'll often spy someone on the side of the road or in a parking lot straddling their bicycle at a dead stop, staring at their mobile device.

At local parks, I still enjoy having SoCal cookouts* featuring hot dogs, ground beef patties, grilled tri-tip, and chicken with plentiful snacks and loaded salads.

These gatherings had *previously* come with a side of legendary jokes and reminiscence of holiday shenanigans. Now they've been replaced with large segments of silence as people browse online video clips, follow trending social media hashtags, and answer random correspondence.

---

*yah that's right, I refuse to call it "BBQ" unless you're cooking low and slow for 8 to 12 hours...

"because science!"

News channel suggestions, social media app notifications, recommendations, advertisements, and alerts are constantly bombarding we who choose to repeatedly receive them, and we clearly have a difficult time looking away. More than ever, cookies, triangulation, and advertising IDs (designed to prey on and fuel confirmation bias of loyalists) are pushing political propaganda, and ensuring nobody forgets to talk with friends about the newest flavor of seltzer, that annoying car insurance ad, or the latest popular celebrity scandal.

It's become a rampant virus within our society.

It doesn't appear it's been good for progress.

Hordes of friends and family who were once punctual and organized are no longer as much.

Back in the '80s, you had to plan ahead to meet at a restaurant, theme park, hotel, hiking trail, beach, place of business, et cetera.

You'd need to establish an exact date, time, and parking location so you could find the people you were meeting up with.

Before the mid to late '90s, only the rich could afford cell phones. Being late or missing was a bigger deal back then because you couldn't call people at a moment's notice and ask, "Hey, where ya at?"

If you were to be exceptionally late on the way to meet someone at a place with a landline such as a restaurant or grocery store, you could *at least* try to call the business and have them page your contact or leave them a message, but even that was a mark of shame.

You'd failed to keep an appointment.

The sting was much stronger back then, and the act of showing up late or not at all was considered far more disrespectful.

It seems to have become commonplace or even expected, nowadays.

Study after study has revealed the overwhelmingly negative long-term effects of receiving numerous, tiny, digitally delivered dopamine hits all day long.

They're effortlessly earned, and don't last.

For many humans, that habit poses a long-term substantial risk of discouragement and depression.

ESSENTIAL INFORMATION AFTER HIGH SCHOOL GRADUATION

Being conditioned to demand instant gratification doesn't bode well for personal growth.

Sooner or later, one may realize that their mood, character, and even *behavior* has changed to the point of not resembling what they'd call "their own."

It's not often a positive change.

When was the last time everybody sat down for a lunch break or a snack after work while talking about nothing but all the positive and encouraging news articles and comments they saw throughout their day?

I can't recall, either.

It appears these "devices" have become more than those of our own, and have left fetid residues of insatiable loathing upon our psyches.

Fortunately, there exists a convenient mechanism for resolving this little development: it's usually a slim, half-inch sized button located on the side of the device itself.

After setting the powered-off gadget down on a table or counter top, we'll have both hands free to grab a container of water, turn the knob to our front door, open it to welcome a gust of fresh air, and go outside into the world for a spell...

Independently, open-minded, and free of the electronic leash that had once been allowed to dictate our every action.

7

Political Parties Aren't Much Fun

They're Apparently Not That Good at Their Jobs

A skilled, competent politician has the ability to unite a body of people, address public concerns, effectively handle the affairs of state, and spur the independent well-being of citizens.

I look forward to the day such a politician might enter any major state or federal office in my lifetime.

Promise after promise, proclamation after proclamation, candidates spew forth their lies and deception during costly campaigns, and bring their sharpest semantics to the table during the lovingly aforementioned *debates* in their attempts to sway votes as desired.

Party candidates constantly declare superiority over the other while failing to actually *deliver* any assured goods once elected.

Paltry amounts of consideration are given to the long-term repercussions of their actions, as their capacity to handle pressing issues is mediocre at best.

Their poor implementations nominally if at all resolve primary concerns, often generating newfound unrest elsewhere.

This pattern is most easily recognized when it affects our jobs, or more specifically, our paychecks.

I'll use the housing market as an example:

Some years before the 2008 housing bubble experienced an ugly burst, shifty business had been taking place within the industry.

Appraisers had been trusted independently for years to provide ethical and accurate valuations of residential properties.

Regrettably, some of them had begun to show a change in behavior of sorts.

A growing trend of real estate agents hankering to sell houses for more than their worth (as to increase their commissions) had resulted in some appraisers being "gifted" a bit of something extra — a little persuasion in order to make sure the appraisals would come in at a certain higher dollar value than their market average would suggest.

These shady dealings were found to have been so frequent and contributing greatly enough to the housing crash that a countermeasure was established by the government: required use of an Appraisal Management Company (AMC).

No longer could a real estate agent or bank directly contact their paid-off crooked appraiser of choice; the AMC was now the liaison that was to nullify corruption by assigning appraisal orders to a *randomly selected* appraiser who'd registered with the new regulated system.

This has only half-solved the problem of obtaining corrupt appraisals, in reality making it only slightly more difficult for the unscrupulous to do so.

Meanwhile, this *destroyed* all the honest and legitimate appraisers' hard-earned clientele, and added more costs, overhead, paperwork, and turnaround time for all departments involved.

There are countless ways in which the situation could have been handled more fairly and efficiently, but that's a moot point.

The government got involved, a flimsy decision was made, and this was the result.

Similar historical examples exist aplenty, thus the *originally* genuine phrase, "good enough for government work…" remains embedded in our modern culture with a bitter utterance of irony and disparagement.

It's not a proud disposition to be associating perfunctory efforts with government performance, but there's an intensely nauseating amount of room for improvement revealed when one removes their political party blinders.

Quite often, the initial actions of a new elect are those fueled out of spite to get back at the previous party's officeholder, punishing them for their conduct and attempting to reverse their *sinister* deeds. This is usually sold with the proclamation that it's for the good of The People.

When The People are convinced of this, their biased, blind party loyalty becomes reinforced, national debt is unnecessarily increased, and voters are successfully pitted against each other once more for the following election.

A troublesome cycle, this.

Our national debt was paid off in full only once in American history, in 1835. The country fell into debt again the following year.

It's rising much faster today than it has in prior generations.

According to the US Debt Clock, our national debt was still less than a trillion dollars in my birth year of 1980. It took *28 years* before it surpassed the 10 trillion dollar mark in 2008.

Just nine years later, another 10 trillion had already been accrued.

Here we are four years after that, and we've nearly added an additional nine trillion to reach the current balance of $28.895 trillion dollars in national debt.

Even when accounting for inflation, that's an embarrassing and inexcusable development.

There's been no slowing it of late, and the only element that has been focused on during debates about the debt is "whose fault" it is.

Fun Fact: 8 presidents have served in office since 1980. Half were Democrats, and half were Republicans.

Want to go back further?

Since the national debt was paid off in 1835, 39 presidents have served: 16 Democrats, 19 Republicans, and 4 Whigs. With few paltry exceptions, the national debt has risen with every one of them.

Still, the blame game persists.

Whichever party's candidate holds current office will be incriminated by the majority of their rival party's loyalists.

The accused will then offer the stale, classic retort of blaming the policies set in place by a representative of the *former* party in power — be it a president, congress member, or even a city official.

The game hasn't changed, and neither has the trend of obsessive spending with only a declining economy to show for it.

That's the *opposite* of investment.

Don't forget that in recent generations up until the early '90s in California, a family of four was able to thrive beautifully with only one parent working full time. Today, a couple with *no* children both often need full-time jobs to cover their cost of living in many ZIP codes.

It would seem the government's routine of throwing money at issues without much thought — or transparency — isn't the best way to resolve them.

I'm hard-pressed to think of a domestic government product or service (outside of law enforcement and rescue teams in select cities) that I can honestly and universally say, "Well, that was worth the money. That's a respectable operation we have there."

They're constantly wanting for quality on both state and federal levels.

(The California DMV, and the United States Postal Service are some blatant examples.)

This doesn't mean for a moment that I think law enforcement or emergency services are devoid of trash that needs taking out, nor does it mean I don't have great respect for those individuals who serve honestly.

It doesn't make me an anarchist, and it doesn't mean I'm a "nutjob extremist" of the right *or* the left wing.

Contrary to what many believe, that doesn't make me a "centrist," either.

What it means is that my party loyalty lies with none, and I'd prefer to hold *all* candidates to higher standards.

Considering the continued hype and buzz within The Media, and telling from the performance of politicians and voters alike, I've long been given the impression that this puts me very much in the minority.

I guess I'm alone in my principles.

We're Apparently Not That Good at Voting

I am a very well-prepared voter.

Whether bracing for a city, county, state, or presidential election, I try to read all that I reasonably can about every single candidate on the ballot.

I don't just read about those with a specific party letter next to their name, but *all* of them.

This takes an incredible amount of time that I wouldn't call recreational.

I spend many evenings sometimes for weeks reading up on every candidate via their official website including their biography, recent activity, voting history, views, and positions.

I then browse multiple varieties of other sources to see if candidates have been connected with any organizations or companies that would suggest a conflict of interest.

Finally, I check for and read about past scandals, if any.

There often are.

In the 2021 California gubernatorial recall election, there were over 40 qualified candidates on the ballot come voting day. I had read up extensively on every one of them before making my decision.

If a candidate has little substantial material available, I'll put forth 15 minutes of intensely focused query efforts before moving on.

If it's a big name who's running, it may take me any number of *hours* to read up on all available material on their official website alone. That's before reading arguments from opposing as well as non-partisan/neutral sources as an attempt to keep any biased reporting in check.

I am a very well-prepared voter.

I proclaim that "we're" as a country apparently not that good at voting, because the majority votes for most every election since I've been alive have resulted in a catastrophic barrage of completely preventable shortcomings:

- An undeniable plummet of our economy.
- A major decline in the manufacturing of authentically domestic products.
- An increased polarization of The People who are exhibiting more boldly than ever their obsession with party loyalty.
- An embarrassing deterioration of quality and value in government-owned or operated services such as public school systems, Amtrak, and that most insultingly deficient US Department of Veterans Affairs. **Our troops deserve exponentially better.**

Despicable character and morality flaws of elects are pointed out by voters of the dissatisfied *losing* party repeatedly.

These voters will then react by nominating a candidate possessing similar or even identical moral deficiencies during the next election.

Said flaws are then conveniently dismissed or worse yet, justified, all because it's *their* party's representative.

This behavior can be spotted in most every election with nominal effort by the unbiased.

Some recent exhibitions are surely still on voters' minds…

An employee of any office (be it government or not) found to have deleted tens of thousands of emails from a private email server that were revealed to contain sensitive subject matter directly related to high profile investigations — would *normally* be in some serious legal trouble.

Alas, the party loyalists defended and justified this behavior, supporting the candidate regardless.

Another contender entered the playing field toting a lifetime worth of numerous business failures involving multiple bankruptcies. This, combined with recorded proof of the individual in question boasting about successfully harassing and groping the opposite sex due to a position of power *might* have indicated this human wasn't exactly leadership material.

Alas, the party loyalists defended and justified this behavior, supporting the candidate regardless.

Wait, there's more!

After using "millionaires" and "billionaires" as scapegoats for many economic faults and downfalls of society throughout many speeches, a candidate was noticed suddenly only patronizing billionaires after having actually *become* a millionaire themselves. When questioned about their change in verbiage, they proclaimed that they had become a millionaire due to years of hard work, as well as having written a best-selling book. They refused to apologize, exposing their shameless double standard.

In a shocking turn of events... the party loyalists defended and justified this behavior, supporting the candidate regardless.

A right fine collection of candidates indeed, each packing enough red flags to make any hiring manager worth their salt send them on their bike.

Obfuscation of the truth, lecherous buffoonery, and shameless hypocrisy have been identified as typical conducts of politicians for decades; this is by no means a new phenomenon.

What amplifies the sting is the unfathomable realization that it's been *tolerated,* and is still commonplace.

Do we really want to continue playing this game of *debating* which party candidates' lack of ethics is more vast than the others'?

That practice hasn't proven fruitful so far.

At all.

As for the mindsets that perpetuate this behavior, there are several illogical gems commonly professed by the average voter that may easily confound the thoughtful individual:

Illogical Gems Commonly Professed by the Average Voter

"at least they admitted it!"

Many politicians have a history of lying, and in turn being called out for it. On occasion, some will actually admit when they were caught, and fess up. When one's own party representative is the one admitting a lie, the loyalist will somehow see this as a shining jewel of morality which foreshadows a future of trustworthiness.

Naturally, when it's the *opposing* party's rep that's caught, only then is it grounds for impeachment.

"Well, everybody has a dirty past..."

"They all say whatever it takes in order to get elected; you have to count on them not keeping all their promises. That's just how it is."

"You have to vote for the lesser of two evils."

What a rather splendid show of defeatism this is, and a fantastic method of ensuring an evil candidate is always voted into office. Why are we settling for, "would you rather eat manure or guano," when there is edible food to choose from?

"You voted third party?! You do know that people voting third party only end up giving away their vote to the other crooked primary party candidate, don't you?"

Ah, no. As a matter of fact, only people who actually *vote* for "the other crooked primary party candidate" will give that candidate another vote. The logic of this one especially falls short being that this line is used by *both* Democrat and Republican loyalists during the same election when referring to, "the other."

It can't very well function in both directions simultaneously now, can it?

"Well, the government's cheating you, so cheat the government!

Unfortunately, the government gets its revenue largely from *The People,* so in reality: Congratulations. You've now cheated your hard-working fellow citizens.

The further one steps back from the bias-sphere, the clearer one's view becomes.

Party's Over

Ask a devout Democrat or Republican to define their party and how it differs from the other.

There's an extreme likelihood that they'll start to list morals, character traits, religious standpoints, and introduce positions on hot seat topics like immigration, prison systems, and abortion rights.

They'll then perhaps insult the opposite party for *lacking* said morals, having *sinister* traits, and holding *different* positions on said topics.

Doomscrolling continues to bolster this routine.

Fear-based propaganda works, folks. Make no mistake of that.

I avoid having political conversations with these people at all costs, as it's a pointless pastime conversing with somebody who seeks to operate with contempt rather than intelligence.

After cracking open some political history books or reading a few articles from prior decades, one can easily identify that the trending behavior of elected Democrats and Republicans is always changing.

Long-time party loyalists have even coined labels such as "New Democrats" or "Fake Republicans" to bring scorn to those who've not behaved like former candidates from decades past.

This is nothing new, either.

So, do tell: What *is* a Democracy vs a Republic?

ESSENTIAL INFORMATION AFTER HIGH SCHOOL GRADUATION

democracy

noun
/ dəˈMÄKrəsē /

1. a system of government by the whole population or all the eligible members of a state, typically through elected representatives.

republic

noun
/ rəˈPƏB lik /

1. a state in which supreme power is held by The People and their elected representatives, and which has an elected or nominated president rather than a monarch.

Other than one mentioning the lack of a monarch, the actual dictionary definitions are *nearly* splitting hairs.

Strange. Nothing about spiritual beliefs, firearm laws, financial policies, taxation, military spending, or labor rights is mentioned at all.

In fact, nothing that social media, major news networks, registered voters, or even candidates themselves would proclaim to define said parties exists anywhere within these definitions.

I know a lot of atheistic Republican conservatives who smoke weed, and I also know a slew of firearm-owning liberal Democrats who are strongly against gun control and abortion alike.

Perhaps it's time to give up the stereotyping and meaningless labels.

It is a foolish thing to assume that somebody who disagrees with a single point of *one* party's agenda instantly aligns with every point of the opposing party.

Maybe the personal assignment of morals and character traits to one's chosen party is more destructive than it is productive.

When seeing the faces of friends or acquaintances who have attended a rally and met or even spotted a candidate in person, they're often beaming like those of star-struck fans who just got a handshake or a hug from their favorite celebrity performer.

As uttered by one such beaming-faced peer that met a certain candidate some years before their aforementioned email scandal, "They were so very charismatic!"

If only they were scrupulous as well.

It's often argued between Democrats and Republicans over who is more accountable.

One recent Republican candidate boasted of their surefire ability to pay down the entire national debt if elected, circulating some manner of rubbish that Democrats have *always* been less financially responsible.

Fun Fact: That one and only time when the national debt was paid off in 1835? Andrew Jackson — a Democrat — was president.

Unfortunately it didn't last, because the country soon fell into debt once more due to greed, and an economic depression caused by the aftermath of a *cough* *real estate bubble pop...*

You know what they say about those who ignore history: They're doomed to repeat it.

Allow me to repeat that.

You know what they say about those who ignore history: They're doomed to repeat it.

Buckle up for another, America.

If one analyzes our top 10 states with the highest debt per capita, they'll find the difference in financial responsibility demonstrated from Democratic vs. Republican affiliations to be negligible.

Texas (a strongly Republican-leaning state) is at nearly $12,000 debt per citizen while California (a strongly Democratic state) isn't much higher at just over $14,000.

Meanwhile, North Dakota (a fairly balanced affiliation) is above $14,000 as well.

Even when looking at *all* the states organized by debt per capita, there's no dominantly shining beacon of responsibility to be found; both parties are rather obsessed with spending far more than they can afford.

Politics, contrary to how many appear to treat it, is not a sporting event.

It's not wise to cheer blindly for a team when people's rights and well-being are at stake.

It's not healthy to combat an opposing party because they've been labeled as irresponsible monsters or controlling villains.

It's far more favorable and beneficial to address issues with true compromise — without completely obliterating all the freedoms of the opposing party for sheer spite.

History shows that when one holds a stance that an opposing party is made up entirely of nefarious miscreants, real progress remains futile.

If people were to entertain even a short departure from the biassphere to observe whether a conflict is truly due to sinister acts, versus an insufficient law or correctable policy, suddenly there may appear clarity of practical opportunity and a new hope in reaching civilized resolution.

Perhaps the first step is realizing that it's not entire parties that exhibit subpar performance, but rather poorly chosen candidates.

I could easily spend the rest of this book journaling failed promises and atrocities committed by *both* primary party elects for President and Congress alike as to dare establish which party has been "less corrupt."

However, this would waste a considerable amount of time perpetuating that pointless blame game. We'd end up with an ever-growing list of increasingly shameful acts committed by party representatives who'd failed to have been held accountable due to political bias.

By that proclamation alone, I'm certain that droves of party loyalists have certainly profiled *me* as they've seen fit, and made their decisions of which "side" to personally file me under.

They've missed the point entirely.

Regardless if one is loyal to either or neither party, the fact remains that significant promises have been frequently made and constantly broken.

For too many decades, roughly 50% of presidential proclamations made during campaigns *and* while in office have actually been kept.

We all know what a 50% letter grade is.

If you were a small business owner looking to hire a respectable and honest individual you could trust to handle and manage your own money, products, and services, would you hire any of the recent presidential candidates, or would you have kept looking?

If you wouldn't trust them running your small business, why hire them to lead the country?

I've found that revisiting Plato's *Allegory of the Cave* seems to provide inspiration to evaluate self-biases often, and to further expand one's horizons.

Maybe next time, we'll all do better.

Lack of fortitude, and unchecked hubris
often result in
lack of equality, and unchecked tyranny.

8

Ethnicity or Epidermis?

I recall the first time I heard and acknowledged the words "black" and "white" being used to differentiate humans possessing contrasting shades of skin. I was about four years old.

I didn't really understand it.
I didn't really agree with it.
It still confounds me today.

Frankly, referring to any humans as one of a few colors based on the infinitely diverse factor of the concentration of melanin present in their epidermis comes off as strange.

What's going on there? Why are we adopting the simple dialects of a stone age human caricature?

"Me tall. You short."
"She black. He white. Me brown."
"We find sharp rocks. We kill big cat."
"Eat big food."
"Sleep much."

That's about how it sounds to me: archaic, oversimplified, and inapplicable.

It's a similar level of personal astonishment as to why many still refer to Native Americans as Indians when we're all aware this chunk of earth isn't India.

Many people from my hometown of the Santa Ynez Valley have European ancestry. Regardless if they're Danish, Irish, or from one of many regions of Italy, their skin colors are *far* from anything resembling "white."

Fresh clean snow is white.

Big fluffy clouds are often white.

THE STAY-PUFT MARSHMALLOW MAN...

Catch my drift?

No human's skin is white, and likewise, no human's skin is black, so why have we embraced this vernacular?

It seems largely to have only caused segregation.

As the border is just a short four hour drive to the south of us, there are also a large number of immigrants from Mexico who live here. Again, many have mixed ancestry from Europe.

As it is with all humans, though it might be more accurate on a color scale to say their skin shades are all varying hues of brown, calling it "another shade of brown" would be an insult to the brilliant array of skin tones of those hailing from numerous vibrant, vastly different cultures.

Go ahead and browse some of the images of the 30+ states of Mexico to get a hint of how plentiful and diverse their cultures are.

Mexico City, Ensenada, and Oaxaca alone are so distinct, they look as if they might be completely different countries.

There is a smaller number of people living here of Asian descent, as well as of African-Americans living in this tiny valley...

Ah, but I've already fallen into an assumption.

Relax.

This doesn't *have* to be a slippery slope.

It doesn't *have* to be a sensitive subject.

It only becomes so when ignorance or disrespect enters the arena.

Lately, some Americans who do *not* have a very dark skin tone have started referring to those who *do* as no longer "black", but "African-American."

Is this accurate, or is this disrespectful?

That seems an entirely subjective question, and as with any other ethnicity or culture, it depends on the context, the intent, and the inflection used.

The individual could have literally been born and raised in Africa firsthand before immigrating.

They could have been born and raised in a country with a history of substantial African migration such as Brazil, Haiti, Jamaica, or Trinidad and Tobago.

It's also possible that they had been born and raised in **any of the nearly 200 other recognized countries in the world.**

This goes for any human one may meet on planet earth.

The combination of assumption and aggression only opens up a breeding ground for confusion, misinterpretation, and offense.

History of bigotry and prejudice has never universally been purely about skin color.

Several European countries have a sordid past of not exactly having always seen eye to eye with each other, despite the fact that their skin shades are all comparatively light.

So, which is it: Are we to refer to people by their ethnicity, or by their epidermis?

Personally, I'd prefer neither — I'm just a human. That's only *my* preference, though.

I've met with locals in Hawai'i who spoke of their complex heritage from Asia. Due to the time their family had been migrated, along with undergoing a negative experience in their original home country during their childhood, they only acknowledged and preferred to be called Hawaiians.

They did not personally interpret nor intend this to be a disrespectful gesture toward their ancestry.

That was simply how *they* felt about it.

Others may feel differently.

Others may not even know of their family's history.

I'm a Yaqui-Iberian-German-Irishman. That makes for quite the skin tone.

Depending on how I may be dressed and wearing my hairstyle or whether I'm sporting any facial hair, my appearance can vary drastically.

I've been referred to, profiled as, and/or guessed by strangers, coworkers, and acquaintances as being Arabian, Samoan, Indian, Hawaiian, Italian, Greek... the list goes on.

I don't take offense, as worse things have happened in life. When I answer them with how I identify, they might apologize or laugh uncomfortably. At that point I'll tell them not to worry about it, and the conversation will progress peacefully.

As for negative interactions, one advantage of being of a "mixed race" is that I get the *privilege* of enjoying a duality of prejudice.

I'll hear any number of insults involving the cultures commonly represented by darker skin, while other times being told I have no right to speak about certain issues or can't possibly understand them because I'm "just a white guy..."

I received the following gem when discussing the economy in a local community group on social media weeks ago: "You probably don't even know what true hardship is. Your last name says it all."

Never mind that "White" is an adopted name from within my recent ancestry, but some keyboard warriors can't resist playing those race cards.

It's a sad reality that there are a great many states within in my own country that I have no desire to visit due to an underlying predominance of prejudice still seething away.

One wonders how many more generations will be taught to hate in this land of the free.

These days, it's largely unacceptable within our society to refer to Native Americans as "red," or to Asians as "yellow." For many reasons, these terms can come with very negative connotations. To me, referring to a human by any simple color possesses a strong risk of either degrading or dismissing their complex, rich cultural history by crudely shoving them into one of five color categories.

The history of racism on our planet is far too vast and complex to even attempt addressing every concern in a single chapter, but there's a certain sensibility that has shown to be consistent throughout time:

Despite accuracy to any color scale, people seem to be a lot more relaxed and amiable when treated with equal respect, rather than categorized as a basic color or even merely another shade of brown.

Humans on Earth are *much* more diverse than that.

As for life on other planets, I have no idea — but I would surely never jump to any conclusions.

The Legendary Battle of the Sexes

As with the definition of political parties, I've asked several different people the meaning of the word "feminism" in the last few years.

I've been provided vastly different answers, some rather disturbing:

- "When I was in high school in the early '70s, feminists were a bunch o' girls burning their bras in the parking lot for attention. They never mentioned a thing about equal opportunities or rights. After a few months, the school finally put a stop to it."

- "All I ever saw from the feminist movement was a lot of bitter girls looking for excuses to degrade men. They were terrible!"

- "They want all men to be castrated and submissive."

- "I don't call myself a feminist; I don't agree that men and women are exactly the same."

- "Psh. Feminists... ugghk."

What was most distressing to me is that every one of these answers and many variants thereof were common replies I received not from males, but from females of different generations.

That's a tragic display of misunderstanding.

Angry juveniles obsessively setting fire to clothing is simply that: juvenile behavior. (With perhaps a touch of pyromania.)

Justifying the universal beratement of men is just good old fashioned sexual discrimination.

The feminist movement doesn't seem to proclaim that males and females should be thought of as exactly the same.

It doesn't seek special treatment, either. That wouldn't be feminism, that would be entitlement.

To demand universal removal of human genitalia regardless of one's sex isn't feminism. It's nothing less than mutilation and a crime against humanity.

If you fancy a dose of the ultra-noxious, look up the assassination attempt of Andy Warhol and the grisly works written by his attacker.

The Media loves to rehash extreme historical examples such as this one, sustaining the perception that radical feminists with paranoid schizophrenia and an obsession with exacting unwarranted vengeance on all males... is the face of feminism.

The disposition that males should be presumed inferior by genetics is not feminism. It's hate.

It's no different than judging a female likewise.

In reality, it appears feminism has never demanded, suggested, or been defined by any of these above objectives.

The true feminist movement appears only to seek honorable essentials:

It seeks unbiased treatment of males and females.

It seeks *absence* of discrimination.

It seeks equality.

That doesn't imply treating everybody in the exact same manner, dictating that everyone wear the same clothes, eat the same food, or perform the same jobs — it means not discounting or assuming one's level of knowledge, experience, talents or aptitude, and not limiting civil rights... based on one's sex or gender.

In *very* simplified terms, it's males and females both behaving like intelligent, polite, mutually considerate individuals.

Falsehoods about feminism are still constantly perpetuated by The Media; talk shows, radio programs, and news networks thoroughly enjoy the ratings earned by poking fun at the controversial topic, stirring the pot.

After all, conflict sells.

They should be ashamed.

There's enough verbal poison within society as it is without The Media getting involved.

In my youth, I'd already formed a rather strong opinion about the opposite sex by junior high based on how I was generally treated in elementary school as a young male.

It didn't matter that I was lucky enough to have good parents who raised me to be well-mannered and respectful, I was still unfairly profiled by fellow classmates.

It's the way of things. It's a rites of passage that reveals your own level of fortitude.

You discover what you're made of.

It all started off with all boys being dirty. They're all *gross* and sloppy. By the young and old alike, girls were implied to always be cleaner, more sophisticated, and more hygienic than boys.

Girls were said to *mature* faster than boys, too.

Though they generally do start puberty at a younger age, and specific regions of their brain do physically develop earlier than that of young boys, this has no guaranteed bearing or influence of any kind on intelligence, social behavior, or emotional development.

Many girls spoke down to me all the same, but as I grew older I realized that had to do with poor parenting rather than the fact that they were female.

Still, some love to hold the phrase, "girls mature faster than boys" over the heads of youths and adults alike.

That's not feminism. That's harmful to young boys' psyches.

Even *other parents* would openly talk down toward me, assuming I held universally ill intent.

One time upon returning to school after a couple sick days, I was referred by a teacher to call a classmate to obtain details of a missed assignment so that I could make it up for credit.

Using the provided classroom directory, I reached out to one of the star students to have her father answer the phone. I introduced myself and asked to speak to my classmate by name.

Before hanging up on me, he coldly replied, "No, she doesn't *talk* to *boys*."

Upon reaching high school, "boys" became "guys" and were no longer just gross and filthy and devious, but had now also become stupid jocks and little perverts who genetically can't help but to think about sex every seven seconds.

Gotta love that one.

That's not feminism, that's a myth. That's not the nature of a "guy," that's the nature of a sex addict.

The only girls that got along with or wanted to talk to me much at all were the girls that were band geeks and computer geeks.

What's heartbreaking was that those girls were heavily teased and mistreated — by other girls. The popular girls.

Mean girls.

After high school, us "guys" finally started being referred to as "men" and suddenly I was presumed by many females to be a liar, a cheat, untrustworthy, unintelligent, a slacker, *even more* perverse, and I very quickly suffered discrimination of recognizable patterns in the workplace.

They were even often verbalized to my face during interviews by both males and females alike:

[When applying for a data entry job]: "We don't get many men applying for this position. Women are usually *far* better at typing fast... Oh really? You spent a lot of time practicing in high school? I guess you didn't want to play football, huh? Heh heh heh..."

[When applying for kitchen prep]: "You want to become a cook? I'll have to see how fast you are at bussing tables first. Men usually don't know what they're doing in the kitchen..."

The list went on, usually revolving around how men are inept at handling clothing, the kitchen, retail jobs, data entry, filing, and other office admin work.

It was also implied that men should already know everything there is to know about cars, tools, where everything is in a hardware store, principles of construction, and general appliance repair. If you didn't, you were often shamed and then asked what you did with your time in high school.

Working many temp jobs in administrative environments, I was often the only male in the office.

It was commonplace for the female employees to rarely make eye contact with me. When they did, it was an unfriendly glance or a demeaning glare that spoke with the body language of a junior high girl, sneering, "Ew, boys are gross."

Shopping in grocery stores as a young man, most female cashiers didn't even look at me, when they had just been exponentially friendlier with a female customer ahead of me in line.

Shopping alongside Kelly hasn't guaranteed lack of mistreatment, either.

Upon replying to one female cashier with a "please" for a bag, and a "thank you" upon being handed our groceries, the young woman made direct eye contact with Kelly and stated, "WOW, imagine that. A please *and* a thank-you? I'm impressed, you've trained him well."

Needless to say, I ignored it and began to walk away — with a smile that grew with every step as I heard Kelly ripping into the cashier behind me to call out her ignorance and rudeness.

As time went on, I started hearing of more *self-proclaimed* young "feminists" in my generation behaving in an even more toxic, aggressive manner. That was what primarily contributed to my distaste for the word.

The reality of the situation was that *they had no clue* about feminism, or what feminists really stood for.

Therefore, neither did I.

I've come to learn that many others like myself were in fact raised with values that already align with feminism, despite not having become familiar with the term outside of its negative connotations within society.

Genuine feminists have always in fact behaved toward me with respect, and yet many have in conversations proclaimed they'd never refer to themselves as feminists!

It seems the stigma of spite, hate, and radical extremism surrounding the word has left a nasty abrasion within the eardrums of both sexes alike.

It takes a great effort to disassociate a word from such strong doses of negativity, especially when they've been administered by one's peers and The Media for so many decades.

It takes time.

So, what was it that changed my perception of the feminist movement?

Their approach.

Intelligence. Respect. Patience. Humor. Love.

The multi-talented musician P!nk gave the image of feminism a bold revitalization with songs that bravely called out not just the behavior of males behaving badly, but females likewise.

She encouraged respect, *self-respect*, personal reflection, and fortitude through track after track of palpable, compelling lyrics. At times she'd also embrace humorous self-deprecation while also diving into richly profound hard truths.

It proved positively infectious, shown clearly through her growing fan base of which was quickly gaining males who were stunned and overjoyed to see the word "feminism" no longer synonymous with man-hating.

Emma Watson soon entered the feminist scene, mirroring similar goals with great respect and humility.

She opened more ears after professing she felt the word had an unfortunate and troublesome history, explaining that there was still much work to be done to remove the misunderstanding that only women can be feminists.

Speaking very plainly and sharing carefully crafted relatable perspectives, she too had more people shedding their disgust for the term.

And then...

Along came Iliza.

She'd actually been around for a few years before I'd heard of her, but I didn't watch a lot of TV at the time.

Additionally, when you live in a town with a population of under 5,000 where locals can be seen walking their goats down the main street on a leash, you tend to be a little late to some parties.

Iliza Shlesinger makes me laugh.

She makes me laugh hard.

I'm talking about fully wheezing, tear-streaming gut-busting *laughter.*

She also doles out several refreshingly positive male-supporting aspects of feminism that crush its misrepresented past:

"Being a feminist means you just wanna be treated fairly, you just want it even, no more, no less."

"...men aren't allowed to have feelings in our society, which isn't fair."

"You can be pro-woman without being anti-man. We have to adjust that, okay?"

Many are trying very hard to associate feminism with positivity and understanding rather than bitterness and repulsion.

Slowly but surely, it's working.

Fewer innocent men are feeling attacked, and more are suddenly paying attention.

I've heard the subject arise more often within the last few years at restaurants, public houses, wine cellars, parks, cookouts, and even board game and video game parties.

More men and women all around me have begun to speak about the nontoxic face of feminism that has reemerged in recent years.

I notice that they too sometimes mention P!nk, or Emma, or Iliza.

If they don't, *I'll* bring them all up.

Rock on, ladies.

The loudest self-proclaimed pseudo-feminists that have long thrived off the attention of hatespeak are being called out one by one — by genuine female feminists.

After all, *they* detest that behavior just as much as males or perhaps even more, as it strongly detracts from their very objective.

As a male, I refuse to accept it as "the norm" to be eyeballed as a predator when I'm the only male in an office.

It's not right that if I'm going to a wine cellar or taproom, I prefer to do so with one or more female friends in the party in order to avoid being looked down upon or suspected by other females as the single creepy guy in the room.

You can *feel* that when it happens to you, and it's frequent.

While conservatively dressed, I'll go for walks at night to enjoy the lights of beautiful downtown Solvang, sometimes alone if Kelly is still at work. When a single woman or even a trio of female friends is walking toward me on the same side of the street, they'll sometimes cross from *far out* to the other side as soon as they notice me.

They don't do that when they pass other females.

Likewise, if on occasion during a mid-morning walk I pass a female of any age in broad daylight, I'll always maintain a wide distance and at times even step down off the curb while making quick eye contact, giving the standard smile and brief head-nod, and saying "good morning" or "hello" as I pass.

I rarely get answered or acknowledged. Frequently, they actively look down or look away.

This is standard, and it's not healthy.

I often hear a phrase from some females looking to justify these types of behaviors:

"You don't know what it's *like* to be female."

With all due respect, they don't know what it's like to be male.

That only means we can't *relate*.

That doesn't mean we can't understand each other.

When I dare discuss the topic of feminism with others be they male or female, risk of bigotry comes with the territory.

"What right do *you* have to talk about feminism?"

"What could men *possibly* understand about it?"

Insulting, yes, but more so painfully ironic since all my expressed views and understandings of the feminist movement continue to be shaped by having civilized conversations with, and willingly hearing out the perspectives of mature, thoughtful, patient women.

Some powerful song lyrics always enter my mind when I'm confronted with such depreciatory behavior.

The song is, "An Innocent Man," by Billy Joel.

He professes his realization that many people have been hurt or suffered mistreatment, but an innocent man is willing to listen and even take a few raps. He knows that patience, understanding, and selflessness serve as an olive branch to those lashing out from having been wounded by others.

These lyrics are easily applied beyond a romantic or personal relationship, and I often try upholding these tenets when being profiled and unfairly persecuted by females.

Consequently, there's a *limit* to a human's endurance of unwarranted vengeance, and a great tragedy occurs when an innocent man is retained as the punching bag for too long, by too many — and is drained of his vitality to tolerate any more.

He turns emotionally numb, grows quiet, and becomes reserved; he stops fighting the good fight.

Just as great insight must be exercised to better understand the plight of feminism, great care must be taken as to avoid driving innocents to silence.

Moving Forward: Confounding Sexism

Unchecked biases over many generations give way to assumptions, myths, and prejudices. Being observant, embracing different perspectives and having calm conversations with one another can nullify these negatives and give chance for change.

In closing, these are just a few of too many common misconceptions to which I've added some insights that may serve as practice to confound sexism and eradicate falsehoods.

- "Men are better at math than women." Does anyone, male *or* female wish to go up against Felicia Day at a Mathematics Competition? She'll enjoy running circles around you with a pencil in one hand and a violin bow in the other — she graduated college in the top 4% of her class with a double major in math and music at age 19. As it stands, study after study continues to show absolutely no substantially innate genetic advantage of mathematical competency from either sex.

- "Those who adopt the traditional role as a wife or mother are perpetuating the exploitation of women by submission to a male dominated society." A stranger on social media dropped a paragraph worth of this drivel to Kelly a couple years ago, stating that she was probably so used to *my likely mistreatment of her* that chances are she didn't even realize she was a victim. To my disgust, that comment was liked by several locals, none of which had even met me. When I dared chime in to defend myself against this person and point out her blatantly discriminatory accusation, she accused me of "mansplaining." Thus, one more hateful term that needs to disappear along with these destructive assumptions.

- "Women are far cleaner and much more sophisticated than men." Since I'd heard this my whole life, I presumed it to be universally true until the day I visited Kelly at her first college of choice. The female dormitory as a whole was perhaps one of the most foul and uncivilized dwellings I'd ever seen. She ended up transferring away after a year of tolerating that putrid living environment. Years later, the discussion came up of *my* disgust regarding men's public restrooms; I professed that I'm the only person I see washing my hands 90% of the time upon exit. Several nearby women chimed in stating it happens in *their* restrooms as well, but Kelly topped them all with her story: She once saw a young woman open the door to a public restroom and dump a large beer stein full of a vile-colored liquid into the sink just as Kelly was intending to wash her hands. It was at a beerfest, and the substance was the young woman's vomit. It would appear *all* humans are clearly vulnerable to a lack of hygiene and elegance, regardless of gender.

- "Old white men" are quite the universal scapegoats for an inaccurately large number of atrocities mentioned by society. This is no different than any other prejudice, and likewise needs to stop. Last year on the patio of a local restaurant, I was laughing in shock after reading an online comment from a friend who raises goats on a farm. They had been discussing the day of slaughter: "Yah, these goats are cute when they're younger, but when they grow up, some develop such an arrogant and ornery attitude, you really don't mind gettin' rid of'm..." Nearby, somebody who had overheard me reading the comment leaned over and replied to me angrily, "A *farmer* said that? That's horrible! Sounds *just like* the typical ravings of an old white man!" I enlightened them with the fact that my farmer friend wasn't an old white man, but a *young Native American woman*. My grandfather was an "old white man." He was German. He was also neither a Nazi, a bigot, a corrupt politician, an alcoholic, an abuser, or a litterbug. (Imagine that!) Further confounding this trend is that I *almost* exclusively hear this slight against "old white men" from the mouths of those themselves who identify as "white." Some would label that "white guilt." I call it what it is — prejudice.

- I roll my eyes every time I hear people say, "girls aren't as good as guys at playing video games." Way back in 1988, a gamer just a couple years older than me was kind enough to demonstrate a detailed play-through in person on how to complete *Super Mario Brothers* without a hitch. *Her* name was Lindsay Everett, a friend of my older sister. Whenever I play through that game today, I still practice the techniques and methods she taught to me. Much later in life, a *Super Smash Brothers* tournament was being held at a local shopping mall where I lived. The winner (who happened to be male) was still playing a few rounds after the tournament to oblige those who hadn't signed up to officially compete. He defeated several nearby eager opponents effortlessly — until he challenged my younger sister. She'd been closely observing his play style during the event, and proceeded to completely wipe the floor with him several times in a row. With a stunned smile on his face, he congratulated and encouraged her to sign up for the next tournament. I wasn't surprised; she'd already been pulverizing me in our battles at home for years.

Some People Have No Class

During one of my shifts at an electronics store in the late '90s, in walked a middle-aged man wearing faded sneakers, shabby denim shorts, and a weathered burgundy T shirt.

Though his hair was untrimmed and his face unshaven, his hygiene was excellent.

He approached the counter, and asked the manager if he could special order some audio equipment.

Catalogs were flipped through for about 10 minutes before the man finished selecting custom audio components for a new home theater.

An impressive albeit modest setup, he didn't spend a great amount, staying well under $1,000.

He was intricately familiar enough with the hardware as to maximize value.

The man also opted to have my coworker (the manager) personally install the system when the equipment arrived.

All went well, and two weeks later the job had been completed with customer satisfaction.

When my coworker had returned to the store that day after performing the install, he laughed and said he had a bit of a surprise when he first arrived at the man's home.

It was a mansion. The guy was absolutely loaded. This had been a *smaller* audio system for a spare bedroom.

Neither of us would have guessed, and we were both guilty of having judged him by his appearance.

Stained T shirt. Tore up shoes. Tattered shorts...

He wasn't wearing them because he couldn't afford new ones, they were comfortably functional clothes and he didn't have to impress anybody.

I should have known better. Earlier that year I'd gotten a dose of class discrimination myself for the umpteenth time.

I was pulled over on the way to the Blockbuster Video in Buellton to return a DVD, but was used to this treatment for a typical reason:

I was driving an eyesore of a vehicle.

It was a 1984 Mitsubishi Mighty Max with a heavily scraped up paint job. The front fenders had been cut high to accommodate the former owner's massive tires which had been replaced with those of standard size before they'd sold it.

It looked atrocious.

It was equipped with a used four-cylinder engine taken from an old Toyota Corolla, so it got a rockin' nine miles to the gallon.

I was driving an eyesore of a vehicle, but that's no crime.

It was fully legal, smog check compliant, had all required working parts and lights, was registered and insured, and I was a licensed driver.

The cop was one of the same two that had pulled me over countless times in my former vehicle (the '81 Chevy Citatio) on account of *it* looking old and neglected as well.

Despite all the times I'd been pulled over, I had zero tickets to show for it.

This wasn't, and isn't unheard of.

City cops will pull over an older vehicle just to see what they can find. From my experience, they'll often kick-start the conversation by making up a lie, saying that the vehicle was swerving in the lane or that the driver was slightly speeding.

The sad fact of the matter is: More often than not, pulling over an older vehicle with rust or dirty scratched paint after dark is statistically quite likely to come up with an expired plate, no insurance, no license, or at least a few random repairs as to rack up some fix-it tickets.

Drugs and other illegal objects are more likely to be discovered, too.

This is not my assumption; this has come from the mouths of several police officers I've personally known in the Santa Barbara, Los Angeles, and San Diego Counties over the years.

Thus, those with weathered, used vehicles grew accustomed to being pulled over and harassed when driving through town at night.

As usual, I was first asked if I'd been drinking. After having the question rephrased twice more, I was given the "follow my finger" test while having a miniature key-chain flashlight shined into my eyes.

The cop dropped both go-to lines, and said I had been "swerving over the lane for awhile back there" and "was going 40 in the 35 zone, too."

Neither was true.

Two of my good friends, Dustin and Blake, had been riding along as passengers right next to me, both safely buckled. They too were asked several times if *they'd* been drinking.

Blake couldn't help but to laugh, being very real from the start of the ordeal and asking, "Really? We're all under-age and it's 7 o'clock on a weekday."

As the cop ignored the comment, he prodded me further, "So you boys going down to race in the riverbed and cause trouble tonight?"

"In this truck? Not likely. We're going to Blockbuster to return this DVD."

I held it up, as it had been resting on the dash.

"Where do you plan to go after that?"

"We'll probably grab some cheeseburgers, get cranked up on some sugar and caffeine, then go back to my parents' house to play video games all night."

"And where is that?"

"Solvang."

"And where in Solvang do your parents live?"

"Right off Laurel, up the hill a ways from Alisal Road."

You see, there *was* no 35 zone on the highway at any point between Alisal Rd. in Solvang, and where I'd been pulled over just before Buellton.

Right then, he knew from my inflection that he'd been called out as having lied about me "going 40 in the 35 zone..."

Still, more banter of belittlement continued, and after repeating our agenda and where I lived several more times, the officer let us go.

No ticket was issued, because no crime had been committed.

Well, other than him harassing us, that is.

This unpleasant ritual continued for about another year before it suddenly stopped. Not because several residents had gotten together and reported harassment to the police departments in the valley — no, no, no. That had proven fruitless.

I'd *sold* that truck and upgraded to a newer vehicle: A '95 sedan with a much shinier paint job.

To this day, I've still zero tickets or accidents on my record.

I'm an excellent driver.

As infuriating as it is, classes are discriminated against by citizens and governments alike. It's a tale as old as time.

Tax brackets, subsidies, The Media, fashion, marketing, and vehicles can all serve as maddening elements that — when allowed — can segregate The People and violate equality just like any other prejudice.

It's not too difficult to confound.

Though the phrase is so trite that it may churn the stomach hearing it again, as with many trite things is absolutely true:

It is unwise to judge a book by its cover.

Of Indignation and Martyrdom

Nobody enjoys being discriminated against, regardless of the method of prejudice involved.

To discount the legitimate suffering of individuals by any reasoning is to deny them of justified indignation.

Recognition of pain or mistreatment is crucial to the mental and emotional healing process of the human psyche; trauma must be acknowledged before it can be moved on from in a healthy manner.

Many have long suffered prejudice and in turn inequality based on sex, gender, skin color, ethnicity, ancestry, age, height, faith, religion, social class, sexual orientation, political views, and other elements too plentiful to mention.

What's worse is that most of these prejudices *have* been acknowledged by society, and continue still.

This is inexcusable.

Even so, there remains another equally unhealthy side of the coin...

Exploitation, excessive self-righteousness, and feigned suffering (acts of martyrdom) have the power to cause matched unrest among The People.

Therein lies the rub: Who is to judge what is excessive? How is *that* person to then be kept in check?

If we're truly demanding equality, why do we continue to be segregated with government forms and job applications demanding our age, ethnicity, and gender?

If it is established that any living innocents are to be held socially accountable for crimes of their ancestors, blood is to be found on *all* hands.

At what point does unresolved loathing and spite usurp rationality and progress?

A step outside of the bias-sphere reveals just *one* human race distinguished by the good and the evil, the foolish and the wise, the cruel and the caring.

We've still much to learn about what matters.

> I don't want there to be gay marriage, I just want there to be happy marriage and lasting marriage and healthy marriage. I look forward to a day where we don't have to talk about it anymore. That's far off. We all want to be loved and accepted and understood, and unfortunately the human race has not figured this out yet.
>
> -Alecia Moore (P!nk)

> Personally, I care a lot more about people who pee all over the toilet seat than I do about peoples' birth gender.
>
> -Janis Ian

> If I were you
> And you were me
> Would we still be doomed
> To disagree?
> 'Cause you'd be me
> If I were you
> And you'd never see
> My point of view
> If I were you
>
> -Jon Foreman of Switchfoot

9

Onward

I can still remember a television ad I first saw in the mid '80s when I was six years old. It was technically a PSA that was still being aired regularly despite having been from 1971.

This one-minute message featured a Native American man rowing down a body of water in a canoe. Random bits of trash are seen floating about and scraping against the sides of his vessel.

With a cliché soundtrack building as the camera slowly pans out, the man is revealed to be rowing outside a large industrial modern-day city with pollution in the air and increasingly plentiful waste drifting in the waters.

He docks his canoe and walks to the edge of a nearby highway only to have a passenger of a moving vehicle toss a bloated plastic bag out the window.

Its contents of garbage dramatically burst open onto the ground in front of him.

The camera then turns and zooms in on his face to reveal a single tear slowly falling from his right eye as the final tagline is narrated:

"People start pollution. People can stop it."

That announcement left six-year-old me rather confused. After all, it had suggested Native Americans to be the only ones that treasured the Earth, and every other American to be universally careless beings who have no qualms about tossing rubbish onto the road and into waters regularly.

Though I had Native American blood from my father's side... my mother, her parents, my teachers, and many friends' parents did not.

They all had still made it quite clear that it was not okay to throw trash on the ground. When spotting it, it was encouraged to be a good example to others by picking it up, and placing it in a garbage can.

Even to a child, it was obvious that you didn't need to be a Native American to respect the Earth.

I didn't realize it at that age, but what was going on was that I was a little offended by that PSA. It *seemed* as if its chosen theme was accusing my non-Native American mother of being a litterbug.

It really wasn't intending to; that was my own personal, *initial* interpretation at age six.

Years later, I learned in high school that the man in the PSA was no Native American. Despite rumors that the famous "Crying Indian" (as he'd come to be known) was Cherokee, he was in fact *not*.

He was an actor known as "Iron Eyes Cody" — born in Louisiana to Italian parents.

Still, I didn't feign resentment or feel like exploiting the matter for attention.

It wasn't worth over-analyzing. I simply looked at the bigger picture: The purpose of the PSA was to bring attention to the despicable act of littering.

It succeeded.

Many people were upset to find out that an actor of Italian descent was cast to portray a Native American, calling it racist.

...but was it really?

His character didn't appear to be shined in any negative light. In fact it was quite the opposite.

Did the hiring director of the "Keep America Beautiful" organization that produced the famous PSA have a history of racist behavior toward Native Americans?

Did any Native Americans actually *apply* for the role and get rejected due to their skin color or ancestry?

That's far too many conclusions to be jumping to, and it would benefit some folks to take a deep breath and relax before throwing so many accusatory darts.

Even *voice acting* has become a target of excessive scrutiny.

Cartoon networks have taken to broadcasting only heavily edited *Speedy Gonzales* cartoons when aired, playing just the music soundtrack with the dialogue having been completely removed.

Some people had decided they were offended — not by any specific dialogue itself, but the fact that this fictitious Mexican talking mouse was being voiced by the son of Jewish immigrants instead of a voice actor of Mexican descent.

Having some Mexican ancestors myself and being familiar with several Latino cultures, I don't feel *Speedy Gonzales* or his dialogue insults Mexican heritage, or drags any cultures through the mud.

In fact, he's a clever hero that effortlessly makes the *non-Mexican* antagonists in his cartoons look incredibly daft.

I've never in my life met a Mexican person who has been offended by *Speedy Gonzales* cartoons. On the contrary, most find them hilarious and like myself are irritated that they've been censored.

I find it ridiculous that so much time and concern gets wasted on such trivialities.

What's next? Based on these same flimsy assumptions and accusations, are people to allow cancel culture to ban all episodes of *Samurai Jack, Inspector Gadget,* and *Teenage Mutant Ninja Turtles* all because Phil LaMarr, Cree Summer, and James Avery (requiescat in pace) have darker skin tones than the characters of Samurai Jack, Penny, and The Shredder respectively?

Don't you dare.

We're human. It's an undeniable reality that we will be inclined to judge everything we see and hear on some level. It's a lifelong struggle to learn what issues are truly of consequence, and what issues have been sensationalized to *appear* of consequence.

Our country is nearly 30 trillion dollars in debt. That's quite a consequence.

People in our own country still suffer backlash from the stereotyping by others coast-to-coast.

That's another consequence.

One resident parks a shiny car in their driveway, and their neighbor *has to* take out a new car loan themselves to keep up appearances.

Tens of millions have gone without sufficient or affordable proper healthcare for decades.

They still do.

More than one third of the U.S. population suffers obesity from processed food addiction while billions of pounds of fresh nutritious high-quality produce are being wasted every year. Stacks of bestselling trend diet books and record sales of gym memberships haven't worked.

Clearly, this is not the way.

Eyes are glued to screens at dinnertime, and exaggerated fictions become facts for those millions of users constantly reinforcing their confirmation bias one internet query at a time.

When just *one* of my perspectives simultaneously gets me labeled as an "evil right wingnut," a "left wing extremist," and a "bitter centrist" based on who's listening, their party loyalty, or what news network they listen to, I can do nothing but shrug.

It's kinda funny, really.

It's also kinda sad.

Maybe someday I'll be able to walk down the street without being thought of as a dangerous individual by a female passerby.

Perhaps fewer people will flock to organizations with an obliviously cultist mindset.

There could be a *chance* parents of the future will teach their children to behave toward others with the same respect using text as they do with their voice in person.

I hope so.

Every day, I put sincere thought into everything I do in order to try making this place a little better.

I also lend an ear to the respectful thoughts of others.

Despite a Bachelor's Degree listed as a requirement, I recently applied for a technical writing position at Activision Blizzard, Inc.

I'm not a "frat boy" chauvinist, I treat humans respectfully, and actively take out the trash whenever necessary. I've also been managing technical writing projects at a senior level for over a decade with an international corporation.

It sounds like they *need* more people like me working for them.

Be that as it may, I was quickly rejected with a form letter within 48 hours, and can't help but suspect that it was surely due to the absence of a Bachelor's Degree.

We're all going to have to step back, and view the bigger picture. We'll need to ask how we can improve ourselves, recover our economy, better understand each other's perspectives, and heal the wounds in our society instead of allowing The Media and our biases to drive each other into the ground.

I've been a small part of The Media the very moment I decided to become a writer.

An ironic development, given my disposition.

Being quite aware of this, I try to keep myself in check by asking if some things would turn out better if I opted merely to remain silent.

I suppose time will tell.

ACKNOWLEDGMENTS

My Wife, Kelly: For always being there for me with love and support throughout life, this entire project of passion, and beyond.

My Family: For love and support, always.

Alecia Moore (P!nk), Iliza Shlesinger, and Emma Watson: For bringing forth positive light and understanding, uniting those who listen with relatable sincerity and humor, and extinguishing fear and bitterness with patience and practicality.

Felicia Day, Sandeep Parikh, Chris Pirillo, and Wil Wheaton: For motivating, encouraging, and sticking up for geeks around the world.

Jon Foreman and Switchfoot: For lyrics that speak from outside the bias-sphere, and provoking thoughts with aims to heal the fissures between all who live and breath.

Carey Hart (HartLuck CBD): For continuing to help me fix myself.

Mattie Rosina: Last but not least... For your kindness to complete strangers from the far West Coast, of which will always be remembered.

Michael is a computer geek/band geek hybrid from Generation X, raised in the quaint Danish village of Solvang, California. Venturing to San Diego, and later to the Pacific Northwest before returning to his hometown, he has enjoyed a fruitful career in the computer and tech support industries for nearly 25 years.

Outside the cubicle, he can be found recording music in his home studio, brewing ale & mead, hosting board game parties, as well as playing plenty of video games with powerfully moving soundtracks.

Always one to enjoy spinning a witless yarn, he's at last fulfilled his desires to spew forth choice fragments of the knowledge and wisdom he's gratefully acquired over the years.

He still misses Saturday morning cartoons and music videos, dearly.

ALSO AVAILABLE FROM MICHAEL ANTHONY WHITE:

True Tales from the Land of Digital Sand

voxgeekus.wordpress.com

www.ingramcontent.com/pod-product-compliance
Lightning Source LLC
Chambersburg PA
CBHW072153100526
44589CB00015B/2215